BORDER MEDIASCAPES

BORDER MEDIASCAPES

Cinematic Itineraries at the Edge of Europe

FRANCESCO ZUCCONI

MINNESOTA

University of Minnesota Press
Minneapolis — London

Excerpts from Niki Giannari's poetry *Des spectres hantent l'Europe (Lettre de Idomeni)* are reprinted with permission of the author.

Chapter 1 is adapted from "Hot and Cold Borders: Sketches for a Geopolitics of Environmental Media," *Diacritics* 50, no. 4 (2022): 48–70. doi:10.1353/dia.2022.a916402; copyright 2022 Cornell University.

Published by the University of Minnesota Press
111 Third Avenue South, Suite 290
Minneapolis, MN 55401–2520
http://www.upress.umn.edu

ISBN 978-1-5179-1890-3 (hc)
ISBN 978-1-5179-1891-0 (pb)

A Cataloging-in-Publication record for this book is available from the Library of Congress.

Printed in the United States of America on acid-free paper

UMP BmB 2025

CONTENTS

ACKNOWLEDGMENTS

I have dedicated several years to this book, discussing it with many people to whom I owe a deep debt of gratitude. I am grateful to University of Minnesota Press director Douglas Armato and all the editorial board for accepting the project and believing in it. Editorial assistant Zenyse Miller supported me with professionalism and generosity during the various steps. My thanks to Matthew Fuller and Áine O'Healy for their readings and for providing me with precious insights. A big thanks goes to Karen Pinkus, for the encouragement and suggestions she has offered me from the very beginning. Lorenzo Alunni and Nicola Perugini accompanied me during the various stages of the work, reading each section of the manuscript as it took shape and helping to develop its rationale. I also want to express my gratitude to Giovanni Careri, Iain Chambers, Roberto De Gaetano, Carmelo Marabello, and Pietro Montani, with whom I shared all this when it was in germinal form and from whom I received valuable criticism and ideas. During the most intense phase of writing, I had the good fortune to dialogue with Francesco Casetti, who read the manuscript and provided me with essential insights. A very special thanks goes to him.

The ideas in the chapters of this book have been presented in various contexts. The conference "La forma cinematografica del reale," hosted at the University of Palermo, December 12–14, 2018, afforded me valuable feedback, especially from Alessia Cervini, Daniele Dottorini, and Bruno Roberti. I would also like to mention the conference "Luoghi, frontiere, ambiente: Questioni e metodi della geocritica," organized at the University of Campania on December 18, 2020, by Elena Porciani and Francesco Sielo. Another valuable opportunity was presented by the FilmForum conference—"And Yet It Moves: On Cinema, Media, and Mobility," organized by the University of Udine, November 2–5, 2021—for which I thank the scientific coordinators Diego Cavallotti, Simone Dotto, Andrea Mariani, Leonardo Quaresima, and Simone Venturini.

Particularly significant for me was the conference "Warburg Migrations: Savoirs, Images, Personnes," held May 30–31, 2023, at the Musée des civilisations de l'Europe et de la Méditerranée (MUCEM) in Marseille, where I benefited especially from an exchange with Sabine Guermouche, Matteo Vallorani, Simon Séguier-Faucher, Emanuele Coccia, Philippe Despoix, Georges Didi-Huberman, and Mathieu Pernot. In December 2023, I also presented a sketch of this work at the Doctoral School in Civil-Environmental Engineering and Architecture at the University of Trieste, Gorizia campus, where, thanks to a discussion with Giuseppina Scavuzzo and her collaborators, I learned a lot about the architecture and archaeology of border areas. Another highlight was my participation in the workshop "On Protective Media," organized at Yale on March 29, 2024, for which I thank the organizers, Francesco Casetti and Pauline LeVen, and all the participants. Finally, I mention the workshop "Le monde à l'épreuve de l'exil," organized by Anne-Claire Defossez and Didier Fassin at the Academy of France in Rome–Villa Medici, May 29–30, 2024, where I had the opportunity to share my research and gained precious insights.

Some parts of the book were read by Luca Acquarelli, Pierandrea Amato, Simona Arillotta, Giorgio Fichera, Maria Anna Mariani, Camilla Pietrabissa, and Giacomo Tagliani, who provided me with timely comments and helped me finalize the manuscript. The dialogue I had with Massimiliano Coviello and Angela Maiello also influenced the development of the sections of this book. Several other friends and colleagues have participated unknowingly in the labor of writing by engaging with me in discussions on topics of shared interest. My thanks, in alphabetical order, to Maria Cristina Addis, Maria Ida Bernabei, Marco Bertozzi, Marco Dalla Gassa, Elsa Gomiz, Stefano Jacoviello, Robert Kauffmann, Tarcisio Lancioni, Orlando Paris, Luca Peretti, Gianluca Pulsoni, Antonio Rafele, Marie Rebecchi, Giulio Silvano, Matteo Treleani, Anna Tuli, Luca Venzi, Antonio Vesco, Kendra Walker, Perin Emel Yavuz, and Massimo Zucconi. I'm also grateful to the editorial team of *Fata Morgana* for all the opportunities for exchange over the years. I would like to extend special thanks to all the members of the editorial board of the journal of cultural critique and analysis *il lavoro culturale,* where, for ten years, from 2011 to 2021, I had the opportunity to engage in daily discussions on topics addressed in this book.

Throughout my research, I was able to count on the support of a number of institutions, specifically the Culture del Progetto Department, Iuav University of Venice; the Centre d'Histoire et de Théorie des Arts, École des hautes études en sciences sociales (EHESS) in Paris; and the Institut Convergences Migrations in Paris. The final work on the manuscript benefited from the excellent working conditions provided by the University of Chicago thanks to a Fulbright Distinguished Chair that I received for the spring 2024 semester. I would like to thank Leonardo Cabrini, Federica Caneparo, Sara Dallavalle, Pauline Goul, Alison James, Armando Maggi, Maria Anna Mariani, Rocco Rubini, Justin Steinberg, and all the colleagues and students who made my stay in Chicago so special.

I am especially keen to acknowledge the extraordinary work of Zakiya Hanafi, who has been assisting me with my English writing for several years. She always encourages me to reflect on the gaps, overlaps, and intertwining of languages.

My gratitude goes to the various filmmakers who have worked in border areas. I had the pleasure of engaging in dialogue with some of them, and I thank them all for their dedication and their productions.

Finally, I want to thank Giulia for all the beautiful things that nourish life and make possible that form of isolation and sharing that is writing.

INTRODUCTION

BORDER MEDIASCAPES

Borders are everywhere. They are the effect of media devices, either fixed on the land or scattered and mobile, capable of tracking the movements of bodies and sweeping far and wide. These technologies act on the surrounding environment, tracing out the geographical space and defining conditions of access and transit. While we might still claim to live in a "global village," this notion needs to be reconceived without any universalist aspirations. Revisiting Marshall McLuhan today, one is less inclined to celebrate the idea that "with electricity and automation, the technology of fragmented processes suddenly fused with the human dialogue and the need for overall consideration of human unity."[1] The metaphor of the great technological sphere, capable of embracing all, must be replaced by a modular image—or one that is "foamy"[2]—adaptable to continuous changes in scale. It would seem that all that remains of the global village idea is its oxymoronic nature: the ambition to regard different forms of life, if not life itself, beyond frontiers and, at the same time, to control, organize, and administer them—palm to palm, formally and informally—as if in a village.

This book reflects on the contemporary geopolitical scenario, particularly European maritime and continental borders, through the lens of media theory. I am interested in the spatial and environmental character of media, especially the close relationship media have with the proliferation of borders and the constraining of routes that migrants use to reach Europe from the so-called Global South. In a post-globalization context, where media technology is integral to daily life, we may have the impression that spatial and temporal distances, along with linguistic, cultural, political, and economic differences, no longer impede our need or desire to move. Yet, beyond the illusions suggested by the idea of globalization, the access and ability to move around the "village" afforded to residents of Rome, New York, or Tokyo are very different from those living in Mogadishu, Juba, or Kabul. Interconnectedness may have reduced spatial and cultural distances, but it has also reinforced preexisting frontiers or traced out other types of borders, shaping new power relations.[3] Accordingly, the decision to focus on the European context addresses the need to narrow the scope of this book's analysis and serves at the same time as a paradigm for the strategies deployed by states and supranational authorities to restrict movement in a region at least ostensibly designed for free mobility.[4] How, then, should we conceptualize the relationship between the apparent diminishing importance of national frontiers and the proliferation and technologization of borders?

In contemporary discourse, we tend to use "frontier" and "border" interchangeably. The practice of using multiple terms to describe geographic and political separations can be traced back to the difference between the Latin words *finis* and *limes: finis* demarcated territorial lines, furrows made on the ground to separate human-made space from natural space; *limes* designated a fortified road or a series of military emplacements for defense or attack.[5] Staying closer to the two English terms, one can contrast the frontier—from the Latin *frons,* meaning both a battle line and the human face, the front end and any outward form that serves as protection and identification—with the border—from Middle English *bordure,* derived from French and German, understood as the outer part or edge of a physical extension. In their study, titled significantly *Border as Method,* Sandro Mezzadra and Brett Neilson examine the differences between these terms. The "frontier" is historically conceived as "a space open to expansion, a mobile 'front' in continuous formation"[6]—referring to European and American colonialism as well as forms of neocolonialism through the idea of "frontiers of capitalism." The "border" has an important "symbolic dimension, which has come to the fore today with the multiplication of the tensions that invest the classically modern configuration of the border as a separating line between sovereign state territories."[7] In her book on the disappearance and reappearance of walls, Wendy Brown primarily uses the term "border," emphasizing the need to define its qualities on a case-by-case basis. Central to Brown's analysis are the concepts of "sovereignty," "governmentality," and "biopolitics"—introduced by Michel Foucault in the 1970s[8]—which are crucial for understanding the changes in contemporary political practices. As she stresses, the design and preservation of borders is not only the prerogative of a sovereign authority exercising the rights of life and death over its territory: "States do not dominate or order, but react to the movements and imperatives of capital as well as to other global phenomena, ranging from climate change to transnational terror networks."[9] As in the attempt to summarize a large terminological and theoretical debate, Étienne Balibar has therefore pointed out that geopolitical concepts resist any form of nominalism: "The theorist who attempts to define what a border is is in danger of going round in circles, as the very representation of the border is the precondition for any definition."[10]

In the light of this literature, I made a choice. In this book I will primarily use the term "border," which I find more flexible and better suited to evaluate the logics used in imposing national sovereignty and governmental practices. It also aptly describes the processes of dematerialization and rematerialization enabled by media technologies. Occasionally, I will also use the term "frontier," mainly to mark the persistence of a historically determined conception of national and colonial space or to avoid linguistic repetition and argumentative redundancy. A geopolitical scenario often resembles a palimpsest where different spatial conceptions overlap and coexist. Although digital technologies have contributed to redefining what borders are and how they function, the old idea of the frontier persists, affecting the lives of those on the ground. New walls of separation continue to rise worldwide—in the heart of Europe, between the United States and Mexico, and in Palestine. Contrary to the idea of walls permanently falling, in observing the dematerialization and multiplication of borders we witness different technologies at work that are explicitly recognizable to varying degrees, intertwined and arranged as an assemblage.[11]

My aim in this book is to explore how different devices function along borders and, as I do so, to investigate the imprint media leave in shaping these geographical and political environments. If I were to summarize this book with a slogan, it would be "the medium is the border." However, I prefer to avoid taking hasty steps or adopting a strongly assertive tone, since both the idea of medium and the idea of border present multiple facets and open reasoning in different directions. This project seeks to develop a chapter-by-chapter reflection, intertwining research from border studies and media studies. Border studies focus on the transformations of border areas and, thus, their geographical, social, and political implications. Media studies, especially in its more theoretical branches, increasingly reflect on how technologies can expand to and intertwine with geographic space, thereby influencing its morphology and redefining access, travel, and settlement possibilities.[12] Some books have already investigated the relationship between borders and technology. Huub Dijstelbloem's work has contributed to the study of the "interactions among actors, institutions, and technologies that constitute borders."[13] Lilie Chouliaraki and Myria Georgiou have explored the datafication of borders and the migrants attempting to cross them, while also considering the legal frameworks and discursive rhetorics that shape social and legal recognition.[14] Other studies, which will be mentioned in the various chapters, have investigated the specific implications of biometric technologies and the way they change forms of social and political interaction.

This book positions itself within this hybrid field of research: I aim to extend the gaze of media theory to fully engage with border studies, encouraging them to delve into the techno-aesthetic implications of these geographical areas. My reference literature is quite different from that of the books mentioned above, and the case studies I will focus on have distinctive characteristics. My case studies are mainly documentary films created by European and migrant filmmakers on Europe's borders over the last twenty years. As I explain in more detail in the last section of this introduction, this choice is based on multiple reasons. Undoubtedly, cinema boasts a long engagement with geography and familiarity with its various techniques and forms.[15] As we will discover, the cinematic gaze does not merely record what appears in border areas but brings borders into visibility, highlighting their multifaceted and hidden characteristics.[16] Through the lens of cinema, I propose to examine the role played by media technologies—from radar to surveillance cameras, mug shots, and biometric detectors—that interact with space and bodies, thus helping to establish borders. At the same time, I will take into account the different practices and forms of mediation, including "radical mediation," that take place between human and nonhuman actants present in the borderlands.[17]

I call these environments, which are simultaneously geographical, political, and technological, "border mediascapes."

A Geopolitics of Media

According to Suvendrini Perera, who introduced the term, the notion of *borderscape* addresses the need for a renewed "conceptual and spatial frame for analyzing what are usually read as disparate elements—negotiations of Indigenous sovereignty, regional governance initiatives, security and border control operations—within it. Cutting across the conventional classifications into separate 'domestic' and 'foreign' policy concerns, the notion of a borderscape allows for differentiated understandings of space, territoriality, sovereignty, and identity across this zone."[18] Prem Kumar Rajaram and Carl Grundy-Warr have taken up the term and proposed a generalization, with the aim of identifying the "mobile, perspectival, and relational"[19] character of very specific geographical and political areas. From this point of view, the frontier appears as a zone of "multiple actors and multiple bodies each calling on different histories, solidarities, and discourses of protection, care, or security."[20]

The concept of *mediascape,* introduced by Arjun Appadurai, is intended to focus on the role of media and images in globalization. Whether produced by private or national authorities, mediascapes "tend to be image-centered, narrative-based accounts of strips of reality, and what they offer to those who experience and transform them is a series of elements (such as characters, plots, and textual forms) out of which scripts can be formed of imagined lives, their own as well as those of others living in other places."[21] While keeping in mind Appadurai's perspective, I prefer to draw on more recent studies, which bring into focus the environmental character of media—their capacity to interact dialectically with geographical areas—to configure and be configured by them. Francesco Casetti, who revisited the debate on this idea, defines a "mediascape" as the outcome of a dual process: on the one hand, "media operate as active agents in the transformation of a place into a space, or of a surrounding into an environment"; on the other, "[t]he role of media is often performed by elements that belong to a territory. A river, a rift, or a peak can mark a space and show up its configuration."[22]

By the concept of *border mediascape,* I aim to integrate various theoretical and methodological perspectives. First, it enhances an infrastructural approach to media by investigating the "cultural techniques" and "media techniques" that shape geography.[23] This does not mean reducing the relationship between media and territory to a one-way imposition; rather, it seeks to reveal the asymmetries that structure and condition borderlands.[24] Second, the idea of border mediascape allows us to focus on the relational and environmental aspects of borders, emphasizing the diverse experiences that occur within them. What emerges is a contested space, situated at the intersection of surveillance devices deployed by the competent authorities and media tools used by migrants to navigate the open sea or continent, document their journeys, send out SOS signals, or attempt to evade the control systems.

This book frequently references the ideas of Gilbert Simondon, who views technical objects from a broad perspective. He examines their various implications at the psychic, social, and political levels, along with their relationships to the environments where they operate. A particularly important concept introduced by Simondon is the *milieu associé.* This French expression stresses that media do more than simply transmit information or make communication possible; furthermore, it cannot be said that a certain medium is found in a certain place. Rather, the construction of a technology arranges a series of positions around it. These positions are occupied by various entities, contributing to the formation of a particular type of environment. At the same time, environmental conditions act and retroact on the technical component: "This simultaneously technical and natural milieu can be called an associated milieu *[milieu associé]*. It is that through which the technical object conditions itself in its functioning. This milieu is not fabricated *[fabriqué]*, or at least not fabricated in its totality; it is a certain regime of natural elements surrounding the technical being, linked to a certain regime of elements that constitute the technical being."[25]

Adopting Simondon's techno-aesthetic thought to our purposes involves, first and foremost, analyzing the agency of media and their geographical impact: the capacity of technologies to impose borders. This concept can extend to what Simondon calls "technocracy," without concealing the dominance it exerts over the environment: "There is a pride of domination in this violence, and man entitles himself as creator or at least foreman of creation."[26] As will be evident throughout the following pages, the relationship between technology and the environment can be rethought and elaborated within a geopolitical framework, highlighting the overpowering effect exerted over individuals traversing a territory exposed to media action. However, adopting this perspective also prompts us to recognize that every milieu involves active participation from the human, animal, geographical, atmospheric, and other agents. What comes repeatedly to the fore, then, are claims to govern European borders by conceiving them as environments that are *stable* or forcefully stabilized through the deployment of different strategies. In contrast to this view, drawing on Simondon's lexicon, is the possibility of viewing border areas as *metastable* environments, marked by continuously dynamic processes of individuation.[27]

Developing a geopolitics of media involves exploring the connections and hierarchies between technological configurations, geomorphological features, and forms of social and biological life. In this book we will explore how certain media assume a geopolitical role, inhibiting or subjecting the elements that characterize a given territory to a regime and thereby affecting their capacity to perform a function of spatial connection or disconnection. We will focus on the relationship between *media environments*—the ability of media to construct actual milieus—and *environmental media*—the ability of the environment to assume the function of a medium.[28] The concepts of geopolitics and biopolitics converge here to underscore the widespread distribution of technologies intended to control and manage territories and bodies, limiting their potential to experience and offer movement and connection. Through this approach, which integrates the various components of any associated milieu, we will identify what always remains an un-appropriable difference. Border mediascapes are as much the effect of governmental strategies aimed at its management as they are of resistance tactics implemented by migrants.[29] Still, they are also linked to the specific qualities of the environment and thus to its specific dynamism and resilience.[30] The composite character of borders demands an intersectional perspective to understand how various biological, social, cultural, and technological categories interact at multiple levels.[31]

Partly because of this overlap between geopolitical and biopolitical claims, borders cannot be viewed as a problem solely affecting migrants struggling to reach Europe, who are often subjected to abuse and forced into illegality. Referring to the title of this book, we might say "Welcome to the border mediascape." This is not meant to be cynical about or disrespectful to those who experience the violent impact of borders. It means three distinct things, summarized as follows: first, the growing importance of borders, both as a heated topic of debate and a stark reality; second, their contradictory nature and the understated rhetoric that defines them, where the concepts and practices of welcoming and rejecting are intertwined; and third, that as the technologies of control progressively pervade the "village," the ethical and political implications of their use concern everyone.

The Media Color Line

In *Those Who Jump (Les sauteurs),* a film made in 2016 by Abou Bakar Sidibé, Moritz Siebert, and Estephan Wagner, we observe the technological yet brutal nature of the border that separates Morocco from Spain. After leaving Mali, Sidibé chronicles his months on Mount Gourougou, living in an impromptu refugee camp close to Melilla, a Spanish enclave on the North African

Figure 1. Migrants attempt to cross the Melilla barrier under the monitoring of control technologies. Still from *Those Who Jump* (2016).

coast. The film is crafted from footage he captured and images from border control cameras. It shows how the imposing fence of separation and the closed-circuit television cameras work in concert to uphold and enforce the border, to the complete detriment of those attempting to cross it (Figure 1). Here, a physical separation line and a system of control technologies work in tandem: the media literally traces the frontier, while these devices enable the prompt intervention of military forces to repel migrants, making the border sharp and dangerous, capable of injuring those who dare to cross it. In fact, immediately after the first crossing attempt, the film shows the wounds of migrants who, once they have retreated to the refugee camp, are caring for one another.

The idea of borders as "in-between" spaces of intercultural exchange, which gained prominence in the wake of globalization, no longer seems fully applicable with reference to contexts like those documented in *Those Who Jump*.[32] While this perspective has enriched postcolonial approaches and provided valuable insights into works and practices that are the fruit of interactions between diverse backgrounds, the migration narratives of the new millennium tell a different story. Contemporary borders are dominated by technological infrastructures that take precedence over the complexities or potential of intercultural engagement. Borders now demand a rethinking of their media components and the power dynamics that govern interaction between individuals, communities, and cultures. In *Those Who Jump,* as in Hannah Arendt's thought, border crossers are risk-exposed bodies who form a "vanguard."[33] Reflecting on the historical traumas of the twentieth century, Arendt argues that each stateless person challenges the legal and political limits of the nation-state system, revealing the paradoxes inherent in the very idea of human rights. Twenty-first-century migrants face challenging and dangerous conditions; they experience and reveal the legal, political, and technological systems of border management. They are at the forefront, facing the growing use of technologies as tools for control and governance.

The reorganization of borders due to globalization processes has been accompanied by the rise of new forms and practices of discrimination. The issue of the "color line"—developed by William Edward Burghardt Du Bois at the turn of the twentieth century to analyze racism against African Americans in the United States[34]—has resurfaced with full intensity, serving as a lens for critically reflecting on the present. In a study aimed at taking stock of how the "color line" persists in the new millennium, Paul Gilroy stresses the importance of reviving the questions posed by Du Bois: "After that 'color line,' then what? What are raciological differences becoming next, in a world where our understanding of humanity has been irrevocably reshaped by genomics, biotechnologies and self-conscious biocolonialism? Is race politics a nontransferable North American accomplishment?"[35] In his book devoted to the notion of "brutalism"—as a new governmental and technological paradigm—Achille Mbembe hypothesizes the extension of racialization processes beyond the communities and subjectivities touched by historical racism, in a kind of "universalization of the black condition *[condition nègre],* the becoming-black *[devenir-nègre]* of a very large swathe of humanity—a humanity that henceforth faces excessive losses and a profound syndrome of exhaustion of its organic capacities."[36] Along these lines, imagining a long-term scenario, Mbembe hypothesizes that "this planetary turn of the African condition and the Africanization of the planetary condition will perhaps constitute the two major philosophical, cultural, and artistic events of the twenty-first century."[37]

An aspect that tends to be overlooked when speaking of the "color line" is the eminently aesthetic and technical character of this political concept: *line* and *color* are the elemental tools of all visual expression, from painting and engraving to photography and data visualization. It is known that Du Bois himself used photographs and graphic visualizations to develop his insights into segregation and discrimination, thus acknowledging that lines and colors could function both as instruments of domination and as vehicles for critical analysis, resistance, and public awareness.[38] Far from diverting or depowering the path of political and critical thought, emphasizing this aspect offers a way to deepen it even further. By making a theoretical and methodological shift from political theory to art and media theory—a key, recurring move in this book—it becomes clear that, over the centuries, both scholars and artists have persistently delved the relationships between "lines" and "colors" by questioning the control of space through lines and the act of drawing in general, and by noting the exuberant character of colors, which break or interrupt the system of figuration, by extending and expanding beyond predetermined perimeters. The entire Western history of visual representations can be seen as a battle between line and color, where line, with its extensive character, continuously strives to dominate the inherently intensive character of color.[39]

To speak of a "color line" thus means to imagine a stroke, a graphic marker, or a physical barrier that separates one thing from another, originally used to divide the population on the basis of skin color. As Gilroy and Mbembe point out, discrimination or ghettoization are not only determined or imposed by a clear line of separation, like a line on a map, a wall, or other barrier. Instead, a criterion of racialization is determined and imposed through dynamic devices that can move across space and subjugate people located in different places, on both sides of what we conceive of as "the line." In the face of media globalization, McLuhan himself recognized the biopolitical transformations revolving around inclusion and exclusion. As he notes in *Understanding Media,* "As electrically contracted, the globe is no more than a village. . . . It is this implosive factor that alters the position of the Negro, the teenager, and some other groups. They can no longer be *contained,* in the political sense of limited association. They are now *involved* in our lives, as we in theirs, thanks to the electric media."[40] On the one hand, the presence of the word "Negro" in McLuhan's work testifies to the persistence of Du Bois's color line in the academic and public discourse of the 1960s; on the other hand, his reasoning anticipates the scenario to come and the governmental character of contemporary borders: the idea of producing separation or ghettoization through traditional forms of containment and rejection as much as through forms of deceptive inclusion. When we focus our attention on the aesthetic and media aspects of the "color line," we realize that lines do not only gather, contain, and physically isolate color. In a global and interconnected scenario, control and discrimination are determined not only by straight lines of separation but also *point by point* or *color by color,* thus setting up a kind of geopolitical "pointillism."[41]

This approach to the problem of borders, in addition to appearing in the many films we will analyze in this book, can be found in some literary experiments of recent years. For example, Shahram Khosravi's book *"Illegal" Traveller: An Auto-Ethnography of Borders* is both an autobiography and an account of the contemporary geopolitical scene as well as a study of contemporary migration phenomena. Khosravi highlights how migrants cope with the borders they aim to cross yet find themselves continually ensnared in a mechanism of "selective surveillance" that mixes, reproduces, and extends hierarchies based on ethnicity, social class, and gender.[42] In another important book that investigates migration in the Europe of the new millennium, Alessandro Leogrande describes the frontier as something dense and malleable, and always there: "The frontier always runs in the middle. On this side is the world of before. Beyond is what is yet to come, and may never come."[43]

Drawing on the aesthetic objects that serve as case studies in this book, my aim is to reconceptualize the *color line* as a *media color line:* a continuous construction of borders on geographical spaces, bodies, and life itself. The documentary films discussed in the upcoming chapters reveal the dual logic of the media color line. On one hand, geopolitical frontiers are marked largely by the media that delineate territorial perimeters. This marking is ambivalent, because while these media technologies seem to intervene on the already established dividing line between nations—and thus appear to simply accentuate it—they also create the conditions that allow a border to function in the first place. On the other hand, once mediatized, borders can be deterritorialized, namely, deployed on either side of their lines.[44] As we will see, borders follow those who try to cross them and, by doing so, seek to control the very idea of movement.

In other terms, border technologies do not merely include or exclude but perform both functions at the same time, on both the inner and the outer sides, revealing the simultaneously inclusive and exclusionary character of such devices. As Roberto Esposito has shown in a series of books on the relationship between *community* and *immunity,* one of the most interesting and problematic aspects of our time concerns the mechanisms through which social and political groups attempt to regulate the relationship between "inside" and "outside." Faced with the irruption of a potential external threat—be it migrants, a computer virus, a commercial competitor, or a contagious disease—the social body responds with strategies that oust or isolate it: "If the members of the community are bound by the obligation to give back the *munus* that defines them as such, whoever is immune, by releasing him- or herself from the obligation, places himself or herself outside the community."[45] Although this is a mechanism designed to protect the community's resilience, it risks backfiring. As in the case of autoimmune diseases, over-immunization attacks and damages the body of society. The analytical efficacy of this perspective has proven equally powerful when applied to migration phenomena and to the biopolitical scenario of the Covid-19 pandemic.[46] While the importance of media in relation to such immune processes has often been underestimated, recent studies have emphasized their role in organizing social and political space. Whenever a screen is in use, subjects are arranged in space, allowing the screen to act as a shield against real or presumed external threats.[47] By observing different devices in relation to their environment, it is possible to identify what has been called a "protective function" of media that continuously attempts to regulate exclusionary and inclusive drives.[48] In line with these perspectives, wherever there is a media device, a border can pass, insofar as technologies facilitate the formation of community or immune environments.

"The line *of* color" can be looked at by considering the objective and subjective aspects of the expression. On the one hand, we can view (skin) color as the object of the distinction and segregation imposed by the (white) line, following Du Bois's critical reflections. On the other, we can investigate color (understood here as a cultural technique and a nonlinear spatial marker) as the subject driving new practices of discrimination, which significantly affect subjectivities and communities historically targeted by racism and ghettoization. By examining the question of the color line in this dual manner, we can reflect both on the persistence of old processes of racialization and on the changed social, political, and techno-aesthetic paradigms of their articulation.

Perspective, Positioning, and the Film Canon

Unlike my previous book, which also explored the relationship between images and geographical and political borders,[49] I have chosen to write this new book using the first-person singular, employing the rhetoric of the "I." This choice is not merely a stylistic preference but a necessity to explicitly convey my perspective and positioning regarding the issues discussed in the book and the conditions of those directly affected by them. My *perspective,* as a citizen of a European nation, includes the privilege of accessing advanced technologies and the ease of moving physically through geographic space by showing my passport. I hope to keep that structural condition explicit in the way I write this book, even as I describe phenomena that influence the lives of human beings whose life paths are different from my own. My *positioning*—matured in the wake of my birth conditions, but also through encounters, readings, and viewings—is that of a scholar interested in film, media, and visual cultures as forms of public discourse and, potentially, sites of public engagement. While I am aware of the profound unevenness of contemporary border mediascapes, I harbor the hope that research, debate, and writing can provide valuable opportunities to take a critical interest in issues that concern everyone, even those who think they can ignore them.

My intention in writing this book is to use films as case studies and "theoretical objects," treating their analysis as an opportunity to explore issues that are speculative and highly practical in equal measure and that inevitably touch on various fields of knowledge.[50] Many of the researches in art theory and cultural studies developed over the past few decades have invited us to look at artistic objects as forms of sensibilization but also as real means of engagement. As Mieke Bal points out, the appeal of artistic experimentation lies in its alignment with a theoretical and critical force that intertwines with and nourishes the analysis of cultural and social phenomena.[51] Iain Chambers, expressing a similar vision, has repeatedly stressed how the arts address certain sensitive issues, such as borders or migration, while also offering an approach to these issues that ensures continuous critical questioning of established viewpoints.[52] For his part, Georges Didi-Huberman has highlighted how certain images that make us think critically do not simply offer a viewpoint on reality but also make us observe that same reality in detail through a critical montage of perspectives, thereby pushing us to *take a position*.[53]

Adopting such a theoretical and methodological approach results in three consequences. First, a book, a song, or a film can be a valuable opportunity to move beyond a self-oriented horizon and decentralize one's gaze, to question the perspective we find difficult to give up. Second, these artistic works not only inform us about current affairs, such as migration phenomena and border operations, but also provide us with a lens or a series of lenses through which to focus on different aspects of these issues, allowing us to reflect further beyond the experience of reading, listening, or watching. Third, the act of watching a film can be intertwined with that of reading a book on political theory, and vice versa. This makes it possible to compare and mutually validate the different aesthetic frames—the filmic shots themselves—and theoretical frames of the social and political sciences.

This approach is reflected in every chapter of this book and, accordingly, in the types of documentary films I have selected as case studies. The idea of "documentary cinema" unfolds in multiple directions and, more broadly, the contemporary film canon is defined more than ever by a hybridization of forms, formats, and modes of distribution and spectatorship.[54] Films devoted to migration and borders seem to be no exception.[55] Over the last few years, we have seen major film festivals honor and give international recognition to films dedicated explicitly to documenting sociopolitically relevant issues. I am thinking, for example, of Gianfranco Rosi—the creator of films such as *Sacro GRA* (2013), *Fire at Sea* (*Fuocoammare,* 2016), and *Notturno* (2020)—to whose work the first chapter of the book is dedicated. At the same time, documentary production has become progressively intertwined with that of fictional and experimental cinema and thus with the contemporary art practice of multimedia installations. This is the case, for example, with the works of film director and visual artist Isaac Julien, especially *Western Union: Small Boats* (2007), a multimedia and performative meditation on African migration. Within this particular process of convergence, we find as many participatory productions "from below"—films made by migrants themselves during their journey—as works produced, realized, and distributed through conventional commercial modes.

A few decades ago, the publication of Gayatri Chakravorty Spivak's essay "Can the Subaltern Speak?" helped to observe and interrogate asymmetries of gaze and speech.[56] The idea that the design of contemporary borders is linked closely to the functioning of the technological devices that operate in such areas is in some ways indebted to Spivak's lesson. I believe that the best way to investigate and reveal the discriminatory character of border mediascapes is to study films made by directors who are citizens of European countries as well as those made by migrants on their way to Europe. Rather than creating a clear separation, it is important to specify the geographic coordinates and production circumstances under which they were made on a case-by-case basis.[57] After all, power dynamics frequently reproduce themselves in unexpected ways: even films made with the contribution of migrants and participatory films in general result from collaborations with European directors, producers, or film festivals where engagement modes and forms of involvement remain indistinct.[58]

Clearly, a passion for filmmaking underpins this project. Yet, this sentiment is not intended to be founded on the illusion that documentary cinema is universally a "better media," ethically and politically, than other forms shaping the border mediascape. Filmmakers who push themselves at the edge of Europe are almost always aware of the criticalities involved in their movements and the addition of other technological devices and gazes to the many already in place—a self-critical awareness whose positive aspects I attempt to describe. For some films, I emphasize their analytical and critical capacities to understand how border facilities function. For others, I highlight their risks and tendency to craft a "spectacular" conception of borders, common in journalistic and visual communication circuits. However, even the limitations of a film, like any kind of research document, can be a valuable resource for refining our investigation.

The following pages provide a detailed analysis of several films, with many others also cited. Nevertheless, this book is not an exhaustive survey of films about migration to Europe, nor does it analyze productions from migrants' countries of origin to delve into the reasons for their journey or chronicle its initial stage. The migration phenomena of the new millennium can be connected to many specific contingencies, such as the war in Afghanistan, the Arab Spring, the war in Syria, the numerous conflicts in Central Africa, enduring militarization and political violence in the "Middle East," discrimination against individuals and communities, structural poverty, and climatic and environmental disruption.[59] The colonial experience weighs heavily on, and continues to shape, such diverse contexts and contingencies, making it an inescapable framework for scholarly and artistic reflection on the present time.[60] Studying the cinematic portrayal of the material conditions that frequently prompt migrant journeys is important but requires a different research methodology. This should be conceived as a collective work, involving scholars with different backgrounds, perspectives, and expertise. Consequently, my focus here is more limited. I will strive to showcase the stories and motivations of those who embark on migratory journeys, focusing particularly on the European frontier crossing and the countless material and immaterial borders that these migrants face.

Throughout the various case studies, we will reference the Strait of Sicily; the strip of sea between Turkey and the Greek islands; the Balkan route; the Federal Asylum Centre in Vallorbe, between Switzerland, Germany, and France; the Alpine ridge between Italy and France; and Calais and the English Channel. Chapter by chapter, a series of theoretical nodes and paradigms of what I term border mediascapes emerges. Most of the films selected here share a common trait: they observe and invite viewers to witness the concrete functioning of contemporary borders. This engagement unfolds as an inquiry into the border, understood as a crossroads of different devices and forms of mediation, or as an intermedial space. Rather than positioning themselves as external critics of the border mediascape, these films inevitably operate within it, thus combining *critique* and *self-critique*. In this sense, they serve as a "diagnosis" of the European geopolitical regime. Film by film, I seek to validate what these cinematic works reveal: what border apparatuses detect, and how they manipulate spaces and bodies; how something continually eludes their grasp—attesting to the inherent dynamism and openness of these environments.

Border Mediascapes: Cinematic Itineraries at the Edge of Europe is divided into six chapters, in addition to the Introduction and Conclusion.

The first chapter begins with a film shot on the island of Lampedusa: *Fire at Sea* by Gianfranco Rosi. This film offers an original take on the media devices at work along maritime borders, and their environmental, social, and political ramifications. Viewing this film through the lens of media theory and border studies offers a chance to describe contemporary national frontiers as a form of geopolitical imbalance driven by media technology. Marshall McLuhan's opposition between "hot media" and "cold media" is reassessed as a key to understanding the different forms for controlling and interacting with migrants who are approaching or have crossed the border. From this analysis of Rosi's film I derive a novel opposition between *hot border mediascapes* and *cold border mediascapes,* providing an opportunity to consider the forms of detection, identification, and recognition in borderlands.

The second chapter shifts attention to the vertical axis that links satellite detection tools to the Mediterranean basin. The first part of the chapter deals with forms of counter-investigation performed at the Forensic Architecture and Forensic Oceanography research centers. Central to this analysis is the documentary film made by Charles Heller and Lorenzo Pezzani, *Liquid Traces* (2014), which reconstructs the events of a stranded boat. This documentary's investigative strategies are analyzed with reference to the history of cinema, particularly focusing on the artist and theoretician Harun Farocki. His concept of an "operational image" serves as a lens to understand the automation processes in border management and to delve into projects like Forensic Architecture, which use images of control against the controllers to hold them accountable. The second part of the chapter focuses on the countershot of the "operational images" by which frontiers are managed, by analyzing *Purple Sea* (*Das Purpurmeer,* 2020) by Amel Alzakout and Khaled Abdulwahed, and *Asmat—Names in Memory of All the Victims of the Sea* (2015) by Dagmawi Yimer. While technologies claim to control frontiers from above, crossing them involves contact with the materiality of natural elements, especially with water as an elemental medium that serves both a communication route and an abyss where traces seem to vanish.

The third chapter moves from the Mediterranean border to the center of the European continent. The name "Fortress Europe" was used by Third Reich propaganda to indicate continental Europe under the political and military dominance of Nazi Germany. In the media discourse of the new millennium, the image of "Fortress Europe" has returned with some regularity to express both the idea of inaccessibility (for those who are outside) and the claim for protection (for those inside). But are we sure that the image of a fortress is a useful metaphor to understand the mechanisms of rejection, forced stay, and "exclusionary inclusion" that characterize the migration policies of continental Europe? What shape would such a fortress take, after all? In the film *The Fortress* (*La forteresse,* 2008) by Fernand Melgar, we observe the workings of the institutional machine at the Federal Asylum Centre of Vallorbe, in Switzerland, where migrants are required to stay while awaiting the decision on their asylum applications.

Following the maritime border of the Mediterranean and the institutional architecture of the identification center, the fourth chapter shifts to the "Jungle" of Calais, France, where thousands of migrants camp while waiting for a chance to cross the Channel and reach the United Kingdom. The documentaries *May They Rest in Revolt: Figures of War* (*Qu'ils reposent en révolte—Des figures de guerres 1,* 2010) and *Fragments* (*Les éclats—Ma gueule, ma révolte, mon nom,* 2011), directed by Sylvain George, focus our gaze on the political character of the migrants' daily gestures and the countless police devices that monitor their actions and restrict their movements. George's films aid us in reflecting on the "natural" and "technological" character of frontier zones and therefore on the eminently environmental character of every border. I give particular attention to the most extraordinary sequences in *May They Rest in Revolt,* where the director documents the migrants' practice of removing their fingerprints. These scenes reveal the conflict between the biopolitical strategies that attempt to fuse the border with the bodies of the migrants and their resistance tactics. The gesture of altering one's own skin and body to thwart biometric identification devices takes place in contemporary Europe and at the same time calls into question the history of colonialism.

The fifth chapter shifts to the border between Greece and Macedonia, analyzing the film *Spectres Are Haunting Europe* (*Fantasmata planiountai pano apo tin Europi,* 2016) by Maria Kourkouta and Niki Giannari. Although the idea of exposing the invisibility of border management strategies is a recurring theme in all the films mentioned throughout the book, this chapter delves into the idea of a "spectrology of the border." The border is viewed here as a threshold, or a frame, perpetually and inevitably traversed by an impersonal movement. The migrants' crossings through the Europe of the new millennium evoke and revive memories of past events, imbuing the border with a complex temporality and spatiality. While the European continent's frontiers are monitored by surveillance devices, and transit across them is contained and controlled, cinema explores their memorial depth. The cinematic gaze acquires an enhanced vision, uncovering aspects that are invisible to the naked eye and highlighting continuities in the discontinuities of different times and places.

The sixth chapter focuses on the work carried out by the ZaLab association, which has organized participatory video workshops in various contexts and locations around the world. Centered on a participatory project carried out in Rome, this chapter explores the conditions for obtaining citizenship as a political and social challenge. By comparing contemporary forms of participatory cinema with the reflections proposed by Cesare Zavattini between the 1930s and the 1960s, we gain an idea of the border and the geographic and social margin as spaces made habitable through the processing of individual and collective narratives. Portable devices and the sharing of participatory cinema techniques and practices emerge as fundamental tools for public engagement and the recognition of rights.

The conclusion reflects on cinema's position in the border mediascape. By reviewing the analyses conducted on the various case studies, I assess the specific contribution that art objects can make to public debate on issues of shared interest. This brings into focus the main theoretical points that have emerged in the book, specifically a critical perspective on political borders that places the issue of media at their center and in between.

CHAPTER 1

HOT AND COLD BORDERS

Nearby Lampedusa

Several pivotal dates mark how Europe's borders have been conceived and managed in recent times. One such date is October 18, 2013, when Operation Mare Nostrum, run by the Italian Navy and Air Force, was launched. The operation's mandate was to patrol the Strait of Sicily with air and sea assets, identify incoming migrant boats, and escort them to the nearest port to initiate recognition and refoulement practices. This initiative was undertaken in the wake of a tragic event: only two weeks earlier, on October 3, 2013, a shipwreck had occurred off the island of Conigli, just off the Lampedusa coast, resulting in the deaths of at least 368 people. Another key date is November 1, 2014, when Operation Triton, run by the EU agency Frontex, came into force, at the same time relaunching its functions of controlling the Mediterranean and continental borders of Europe. Since 2018, Frontex's Operation Themis has taken over from Triton, targeting border surveillance with the goal of stopping migration. These efforts accompany important epistemic, perceptual, and operational transformations that affect how these geographical and political apparatuses function. Despite the obvious challenges these operations faced from the outset, the transition from Mare Nostrum to Triton and Themis marks a progressive shift from an at least ostensibly humanitarian approach to an explicitly security-focused idea of the border.[1]

This chapter uses the award-winning and critically acclaimed documentary *Fire at Sea* (*Fuocoammare,* 2016) by Gianfranco Rosi as its case study. The film was shot on the island of Lampedusa while these operations and their defining protocols were being formulated. Instead of interpreting it solely as a representation of the sensitive topic of migration, depicted with varying degrees of empathy and engagement, I want to stress the importance of also viewing *Fire at Sea* as an examination of the technological management of the sea between Italy and Libya, near Lampedusa.[2] *Fire at Sea* shows the technologies operating along the national borders and investigates their environmental, social, and political effects, along with forms of intersubjective recognition. As highlighted in philosophical debate from Emmanuel Levinas, through Axel Honneth, to Judith Butler, recognition involves the potential to establish relationships based on reciprocity or, conversely, relationships that are deeply unbalanced and discriminatory toward those who are perceived and represented as "other."[3] My main hypothesis is that *Fire at Sea* serves as an analytical and critical investigation into different forms of detecting, identifying, and recognizing migrants.[4] The quality of these relationships is shaped by devices conceived for border management or originally designed for other purposes but now integrated into these media and political systems. At the same time, the film invites us to consider the natural elements (water, fire, earth, air, ether) as media potentially capable of connecting distant places. This observation is particularly significant, considering that migrants often encounter political barriers erected at or near sea basins, mountains, and other physical geographic thresholds. The strategic aspect of this coincidence is often obscured in public discussion, creating the false impression that boundaries are natural—a misconceived "naturalness" that needs to be deconstructed.

The second section of this chapter examines Rosi's focus on media devices that distinguish spaces as either hospitable or inhospitable. The long-discussed opposition between "hot media" and "cold media," originating with Marshall McLuhan, is reassessed to shed light on the various methods of monitoring and interacting with migrants who approach or have crossed a border. The third section, taking its cue from the film's title, underscores the cinematographic heritage Rosi references, spanning the Tyrrhenian cinema of Italian director Francesco De Robertis to the Atlantic works of the master filmmaker Jean Epstein. This is where a second aspect of the border mediascape emerges: the Mediterranean frontier is closely tied to the medial qualities of the natural environment, with the sea acting as both surface and abyss, a thoroughfare that is simultaneously vital and lethal. The fourth section combines reflections on devices used in border media and in the history of cinema, focusing on a specific shot from *Fire at Sea*. In this sequence, a migrant wrapped in an isothermal blanket looks directly into the camera, uniting the visual rhetoric of mug shots, the portraiture genre in Western painting, and a gesture that violates the grammar of fictional films.

The Temperature of the Border

Fire at Sea met with appreciation from insiders and viewers across various cultural, social, and political spheres immediately after its presentation at the 2016 Berlin International Film Festival. The success of Rosi's film undoubtedly lies in its portrayal of migrants arriving on the island and the daily life of a young boy named Samuele and his Lampedusa fisherman family, without lapsing into simplifications or analogies.[5] This is a qualified success, however, if one takes into account a major criticism that accuses the film of spectacularizing the rescues and not giving a voice to the migrants themselves.[6] I do not intend to dwell on Samuele's childhood games and his maritime apprenticeship, both of which have been amply covered in public discussion about the film.[7] Nor will I focus on the parallel lives and forms of solidarity between the migrants and the island's residents—a theme that surfaces repeatedly in *Fire at Sea* and can be found, for example, in Jakob Brossmann's *Lampedusa in Winter* (*Lampedusa im Winter,* 2015). Rather than focusing on the characters, I will approach these aspects indirectly by discussing the technological objects and geographic spaces shown in the film. My emphasis will be on a crucial element that has curiously passed unnoticed in the main critical responses to *Fire at Sea*.

Throughout the film, Rosi constantly shows media devices in action: the huge radar station on the western tip of Lampedusa; the SOS launched from the drifting boats and picked up by the captain's office (Figure 2); the traditional telephone through which Signora Maria asks the local radio station for the old song *Fire at Sea* as a dedication to her son Nello; Mimmo's radio station, which broadcasts the music across the island; the photographic

Figure 2. Remote interactions between migrants approaching the border and authorities conducting patrol operations. Still from *Fire at Sea* (2016).

shots documenting the initial registering of the landed migrants; the lighthouse on the tip of the Levant and the beam of light from the sea urchin fisherman's flashlight; the phone booths for intercontinental calls; and the observation monitors from the patrol helicopters. Additionally, there is the ultrasound monitor showing a future mother her twin fetuses who, like her, survived the crossing; and, at the end, the computer where Dr. Pietro Bartolo has stored images and memories of deaths and rescues from his many years of activity on the island.[8]

By cinematographically reframing the radar and navy control monitors, Rosi explores the spatial and geographical context in which such media are placed and which they, in turn, help to define. In other words, the film reframes both the border management technologies and their context—or, more precisely, their field of projection and action—the effects of their agency on the surroundings, creating a very specific environment. It shows how these technological devices not only represent external phenomena and spaces but also perform a series of operations, generating real milieus that influence the individual and collective behaviors of both migrants and island residents.[9] In doing so, Rosi examines the border as an assemblage of technologies and forms of interaction, each with distinct histories and functions: both new technologies that detect migrants from long distances and old forms of identification, recognition, registration, and control, such as body searches, medical examinations, and all forms of assistance or physical rejection. Indeed, each device active in border areas is characterized by the quantity and quality of information it can process, producing different forms of relationships.

As the narrative of *Fire at Sea* unfolds, the film explores the different "temperatures" of the media that act on and delineate the border. It demonstrates the enduring presence of both "hot media" and "cold media" in constructing the border mediascape. According to McLuhan,

> A hot medium is one that extends one single sense in "high definition." High definition is the state of being well filled with data. A photograph is, visually, "high definition." A cartoon is "low definition," simply because very little visual information is provided. Telephone is a cool medium, or one of low definition, because the ear is given a meager amount of information. And speech is a cool medium of low definition, because so little is given and so much has to be filled in by the listener. On the other hand, hot media do not leave so much to be filled in or completed by the audience. Hot media are, therefore, low in participation, and cool media are high in participation or completion by the audience.[10]

As is well known, McLuhan used this thermal metaphor to distinguish media by the type of information in the message and the degree of participation required from the recipient. Accordingly, McLuhan's differentiation between high and low definition should not be interpreted simplistically in a technological or industrial sense but in reference to the level of sensorial stimulation experienced by the observer.[11] For example, a radar image has lower definition than a traditional photograph and, of course, much lower definition than direct visual observation. In *Fire at Sea* we observe the medium of photography at work (see Figure 7), which can certainly be classified as hot media due the high definition of its iconic data and the perceptual and cognitive feedback it provides. *Fire at Sea* also highlights radar images and SOS messages launched from drifting boats. These are highly sophisticated yet "low-definition" technologies because they function over long distances and particularly because to interpret the data they capture requires complex cartographic and computer calculations rather than allowing immediate perceptual recognition.

In *Fire at Sea,* the expression of cold and hot media in border areas is conveyed through specific compositional choices that highlight their differences and the distinct forms of spatiality they construct. To observe how cold media functions, Rosi often uses shots that feature a technological interface in the foreground, allowing viewers to perceive or infer the space of action and interaction of these instruments through the depth of field (Figure 2). For hot media, the framing is set close to the bodies of the subjects interacting with each other, with or without the mediation of technological instruments (Figures 3 and 4). Rosi's framing of these interactions illustrates how McLuhan's theory can be usefully repurposed for today's geopolitical scenario, creating a new distinction between *hot border mediascapes* and *cold border mediascapes.* Like the media studied by McLuhan, the technological devices operating along borders are based on different modes of definition, interpretability, and information-processing capacity. More explicitly, border management devices design this particular space and the ways in which forms of exclusion and inclusion are practiced within it. This is how the issue of temperature, which mostly remains a metaphor in media theory, now defines a concrete variety of management modes, encompassing various forms of reception and welcome.

The "hotter" the detection technologies, which create high-definition images to identify and recognize migrants by their features, the more vital it becomes to reduce the perceptual distance, ensuring greater closeness. In addition to the explicitly thematized examples of reportage and mug photography in the film, there are health assistance services provided by governmental and nongovernmental organizations that operate in close contact with migrants. If we adopt the idea that any form of interaction between humans or nonhumans constitutes a form of mediation, then the physical touch between public security agents

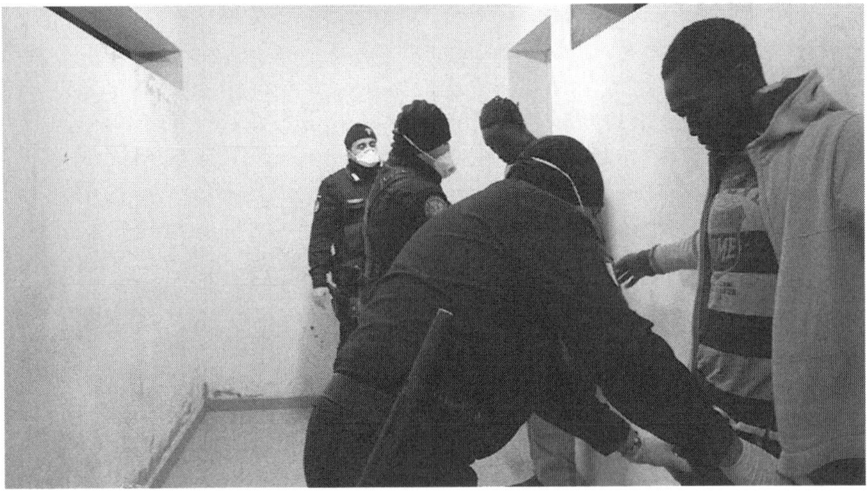

Figure 3. Searches and physical contact between public security agents and migrants. Still from *Fire at Sea* (2016).

and the migrants, who are subjected to systematic searches (Figure 3), results in a high-definition and decidedly hot perception.[12] Fundamentally, a hot border mediascape provides a wide range of practices and interactions for reception, control, and rejection. Despite their differences, these practices share a common feature in this context: the physical proximity and perceptual contact between those who have crossed or are about to cross the border, and those already at the border or coming from behind it.

The "colder" the detection technologies, the less relevant spatial and geographical proximity will be, making the actual crossing of the physical border by the migrant a secondary aspect. Through radar, satellite technologies, infrared cameras, and other types of sensors that require powerful digital tools to be interpreted, drifting boats or migrants' bodies can be captured even over long distances, in conditions of absolute perceptual invisibility.[13] This involves an extension of the potential for intervention and rescue, but also results in an indefinite and somewhat arbitrary extension of control. As the opening sequence of Rosi's film suggests, the smooth surface of the Mediterranean is divided into specific spheres of military and political competence:

from NATO-controlled areas, the Malta search-and-rescue zone, to the Italian search-and-rescue area, among others. Although border management technologies can detect a vessel's presence and track its movement from one area of competence to another in the Mediterranean Sea, detection does not necessarily lead to a prompt rescue intervention. This aspect, highlighted in Rosi's film, is also evident in many other films about migration and in the audiovisual projects made by Forensic Architecture and Forensic Oceanography, which will be discussed in chapter 2 of this book.

Consequently, *hot borders* are where travelers or migrants must cross a visible line or border wall under the watchful eyes of border patrol or the surveillance of control devices. This involves the idea of the border as a physical barrier. In contrast, *cold borders* are active even when the migrant does not explicitly cross a line or a wall identifiable as "the frontier." This perspective views the border as capable of capturing migrant bodies at a distance and determining modalities of access or rejection. It represents the most markedly governmental version of border management, where technologies such as radar, drones, thermic cameras, and biometric data processors enable the authorities responsible for maritime surveillance to decide on their own interventional methods, based on strategic and economic considerations.[14]

First and foremost, then, *Fire at Sea* is a reflection on the ways technological devices not only exist on the border of Mediterranean Europe but also help shape and determine its different operational modes. The distinction between hot and cold border mediascapes helps to describe and clarify the way border environments are built and function, allowing us to critically examine the political implications of these geographical areas. This heuristic distinction helps us understand, at the level of media environments, an aspect already well-established in research on geography and cultural techniques: both abstract and figurative representations play different roles in designing geographic space and establishing how different subjects access and experience it. This distinction between different media temperatures is useful for highlighting that however "cold" the technologies of frontier management may be, borders tend to remain "hot" due to the

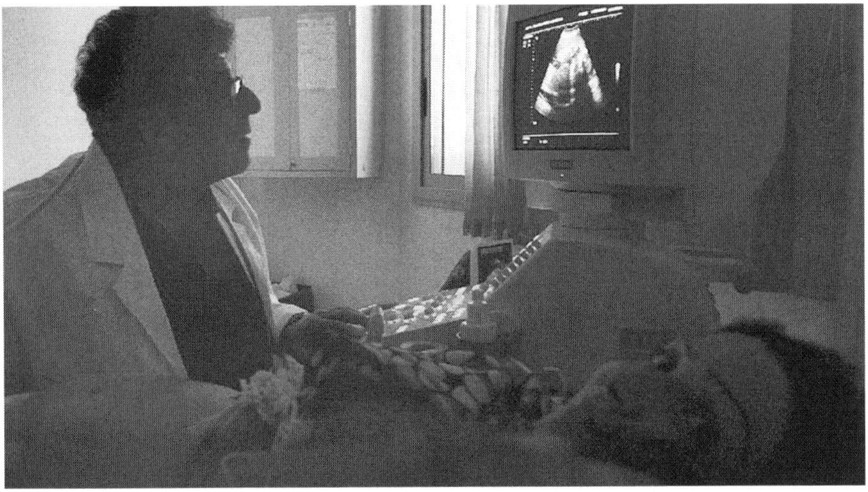

Figure 4. Dr. Pietro Bartolo performs an ultrasound as the results appear on a nearby screen—an intertwining of technologically mediated imaging and physical examination. Still from *Fire at Sea* (2016).

ongoing physical practices stemming from close contact between migrants, rescuers, and the military.

Rosi's reflection extends beyond the activities of the Italian Navy and other authorities conducting rescues on the open sea. At a certain point in the film, a particular technological device takes center stage and a leading role. We find ourselves inside the clinic of Dr. Pietro Bartolo, the island doctor who later became a member of the European Parliament after the film's resounding success. In the foreground, the camera focuses on the face and body of a woman lying on the doctor's examination bed, with the doctor and the technological device used to examine the patient in the background (Figure 4). We are watching an ultrasound scan of a pregnant woman who recently arrived in Lampedusa. The doctor informs her that she is carrying twins. The camera captures his gestures as he moves the sensor to assess the fetuses' health and gender. On the right side, we can see the screen with the image of the fetuses. In this interaction between the doctor and the woman, the rigid opposition between cold and hot media seems to soften, as does the difference between forms of detection, identification, and mutual recognition that operate at a great distance versus others that operate more closely. Like radar images, the "low-definition" images on the screen require sophisticated technology and the expertise of a technician to interpret. Just as in a "high-definition" search, Dr. Bartolo's hands make contact with the patient's body, establishing an intellectual and emotional connection during the medical examination. This film sequence fully expresses the complex relationship between technologies of detection and forms of recognition.[15] The process of scanning at a distance, offered by cold media, does not work here to identify the subject as an "approaching migrant" and then trigger a protocol of reception or rejection. Instead, the cold medium is intertwined with the "hot" quality of the medical examination to recognize and support the development and birth of a new life.

Various studies have shown that the condition of pregnant women can be a potential element of discrimination or control. This applies throughout the entire migration journey, including border crossings and encounters with medical authorities who provide health care.[16] Despite these risks and complex issues, I want to emphasize that in this sequence technologies that act at a distance and forms of mediation based on proximity and perceptual feedback tend to intertwine in a new assemblage. This assemblage is neither "hot" nor "cold" but underscores the ethical value of medical care and the significance of birth. Here, high- and low-definition technologies are reconfigured affirmatively, enhancing the scientific, emotional, and therefore political potential of both hot and cold border mediascapes.[17]

Elemental Cinema

There is something in Rosi's film that evokes the history of cinema, especially the 1930s and 1940s, when the aquatic element was fully embraced on the big screen as a direct challenge to humanity, its technologies, and its claim to control and dominate the planet.[18]

By adopting the point of view of uniformed men who follow emergency protocols to investigate both the surface and depths of the water, *Fire at Sea* enters into a fruitful yet uncomfortable relationship with the cinema of Francesco De Robertis—an Italian director who worked under the Fascist regime and mentored Roberto Rossellini, created films such as *Mines in Sight* (*Mine in vista,* 1939), *Men on the Sea Floor* (*Uomini sul fondo,* 1941), and *Alfa Tau!* (1942). The first is a documentary filmed aboard a fishing boat on mine-watching duty, while the latter two are fictional films set in an Italian submarine under emergency conditions: *Men on the Sea Floor* involves a collision with a ship, and *Alfa Tau!* depicts combat against the British fleet during World War II. As Stefania Parigi points out, "These are war films that, while moving in the Fascist ideological orbit, reject its rhetorical and celebratory style in favor of a look at the more everyday aspects of military life."[19] In the *ventennio* the sea must be marked as "ours," yet De Robertis's vision of a sea battle is less about military enemies vying for supremacy than a fight between technologically equipped humans and the sea. His cinema portrays the maritime experience along two contrasting lines. The first is horizontal: the table where the commanders of *Men on the Sea Floor* spread out their navigation charts; and the sea's surface, where motorboats leave foamy trails, as seen in *Alfa Tau!* The second is vertical: a magnetic force pulling the metal body of the submarines into the depths. Mapping the surface and its navigability does not fully define the relationship with the sea and its control: the sea is both a plane and a progressively thickening mass.[20]

As mentioned in the second section of this chapter, *Fire at Sea* has drawn criticism for the relationship it creates between Rosi's camera, the military authorities, and the institutional migration machine.[21] However, no previous study has noted the potential link with De Robertis's marine cinema. Of course, while the intertextual reference to *Mines in Sight, Men on the Sea Floor,* and *Alfa Tau!* is not explicit in *Fire at Sea,* this juxtaposition brings to light the critical issues in Rosi's film, especially the relationship between the cinema machine and the military and institutional rescue apparatus. Rosi's rekindling of cinematographic memory should prompt us to reflect on the problematic proximity of his gaze with that of the organizations operating on the borders of Mediterranean Europe, the very organizations that facilitated the filming on their boats and inside their service facilities.[22]

Figure 5. Professionals assisting a helicopter taking off from a boat—or the "spectacle" of patrol and rescue operations in the Mediterranean. Still from *Fire at Sea* (2016).

To begin with, given his privileged point of view and the scenic character of many of the shots (Figure 5), Rosi risks taking part in what Nicholas De Genova and later Paolo Cuttitta critically term "the border spectacle."[23] Second, it is fair to point out that the film does not adopt a participatory approach; nor does it directly involve migrants in its creation and execution. Their agency consists in their determination to follow their paths and their motivations to undertake a voyage far from home, which the camera strives to capture and transmit—for example, in the night scene when the migrants sing about the hardships of their journey. Third, *Fire at Sea*'s perspective remains confined within the border mediascape as shaped by European institutions. The film shows us approaching migrant barges (Figure 6) and the media technologies used by military authorities to patrol and intervene in the Mediterranean. However, it does not delve into the specific functions of these interventions. Are they for humanitarian purposes or security protocols? Does this technologization of borders serve to ensure prompt intervention, assistance, and reception for those crossing? Or does it merely serve the securitization of borders?

Figure 6. An overcrowded boat floats on calm waters, reflecting the sea's role as both a connective surface and an abyss. Still from *Fire at Sea* (2016).

Meanwhile, in evaluating both the limits and the potential of the film, Rosi's gaze is not embedded in the governmental frame. Instead of adopting the migrant's point of view—which cannot be his own, of course—or producing an external critique of "Fortress Europe," Rosi immerses himself inside the current border mediascape, allowing the cinematographic machine to engage dialectically with the machines of border management. His gaze is aimed at detailing and fostering understanding of the mechanisms that regulate borders. What some interpretations of the film have missed is that *Fire at Sea* provides an opportunity to show how Europe detects, identifies, and either recognizes or refuses to recognize migrants. It compels us to listen to the migrants' emergency messages and reveals how control authorities remotely monitor their movements.[24] It makes us reflect on the parallel paths of those who land on the island and those who reside there, highlighting the mechanisms that prevent their encounter and mutual recognition. In other words, *Fire at Sea* testifies to a geopolitical imbalance that is caused not by the sea, which both unites and separates shores, but by the technological infrastructure separating the European and African coasts.

The memory evoked by *Fire at Sea* extends beyond Italian cinema from the 1930s and 1940s and its ideological critiques, however. The film's title comes from a Sicilian folk song about the bombing of an Italian warship during World War II. Additionally, although often overlooked, *Fire at Sea* references the history of cinema and alludes to the work of a master of the seventh art: *The Fires of the Sea* (*Les feux de la mer,* 1948) by Jean Epstein. This film, often associated with the better-known *The Storm Tamer* (*Le tempestaire,* 1947), was made for the UN's International Convention for the Protection of Human Life at Sea in 1948. It is an experimental documentary about the Jument lighthouse, located on the island of Ouessant in Brittany, depicting the handover between two generations of lighthouse keepers and emphasizing the importance of maintaining technological equipment and updating skills. Much like his famous ascent up the slopes of Mount Etna, where Epstein realizes that the cinematic gaze is both external and internal to what it represents,[25] the challenge of the open sea affords the director an opportunity to explore the limits of the phenomenological experience and technological mediation. In other words, Epstein conceives of the open sea as a source of fear as well as a challenge to the claim of control: a "fear that demands we do what we fear to do."[26] As has been noted, for Epstein the "ocean's forcefulness, unpredictability, and reign over humankind position it as an ultimate cinematic subject," to which the director is called to answer by "spending long periods of time with the sea."[27] In a similar vein, Rosi spent long periods on Lampedusa, as if a maritime apprenticeship were necessary for making a film in the heart of the Mediterranean.[28] The notions of apprenticeship and adaptation perhaps best signal how to understand the role of Lampedusa's residents in the film. Their lives do not simply run parallel to the rescue operations at sea. Instead, the daily actions of those living on this strip of land in the middle of the Mediterranean are depicted as an ongoing interaction with their environment. This is made explicit by the young Samuele, who, by dint of covering his eye with his hand to play with a slingshot, ends up with a lazy eye, as if to say that living on Lampedusa always means learning to see up close and from a distance, to perceive from within and comprehend from without. Even the silent, mysterious figure of the sea urchin fisherman diving into deep waters serves to illustrate an opposition between how island residents inhabit their environment and how border areas are managed by authorities.

A crucial aspect to emphasize is the relationship between physical boundaries—such as the Strait of Sicily—and the technologies that operate in their proximity. How can radar, radio, and video cameras stem the force of the waves and ensure control despite the sea's abyssal depths? Bringing the question of border mediation back to its elemental character, how can fire illuminate and "heat" the temperature of the water? Conversely, how can the sea mitigate the risks of combustion and fire that threaten every boat, outposts on rocks, the island architecture, and structures on land? Is there a way for technologies to nurture the environment and its ability to connect distant places and communities, rather than serve as tools of repulsion and rejection? Beyond the metaphorical character of these issues, what emerges from the comparison with the films by De Robertis and Epstein is the fact that *Fire at Sea* can be interpreted as an investigation of the tense relationship between political geography and physical geography. From this perspective, it does not suffice to analyze the capacity of media (screens, surveillance cameras, radar, etc.) to create real environments where subjects act according to certain regulatory codes. Instead, we must recognize that the natural elements can be viewed as a series of media forms. As has been noted by John Durham Peters, long before the advent of satellite navigation, the arrangement of the stars guided sailors; water has always been an essential infrastructure for connection and communication, while fire can be considered "our premier instrument of habitat conversion, and one of our most important elemental media."[29]

In *Fire at Sea,* as in Epstein's *The Fires of the Sea,* made shortly after World War II ended, there is a tension between technologically equipped humans and the environment. The transfer of knowledge between generations and the upkeep of navigation and signaling instruments must be ensured, just as it was in the past. Rosi, too, shows us the dual nature of the border mediascape: technological instruments can serve as both expulsion and rescue, and the maritime environment is both a source of danger and a natural connection and route for transit. This perspective allows us to conceive of Europe's border mediascape beyond the dichotomy of "nature" versus "technique." During their journey, migrants face and overcome both human-made and elemental obstacles. However, the hybrid character of the border should not allow the dramatic events occurring regularly during the voyage to be normalized or accepted. Instead, it highlights how the design of technologies transforms geographical separations into power relationships between those on different shores. On one hand, the sea, rivers, and mountains create separations between two shores, two banks, or two ridges. On the other, as Gilbert Simondon highlights in his reflection on the structure of associated milieux, techniques—whether architectural or media—relate to the "key-points" of geographic space and work on their reconfiguration:

> In such a network of key-points, of high-places, there is a primitive lack of distinction between human reality and the reality of the objective world. These key-points are real and objective, but they are that by which the human being is immediately bound to the world, both in order to be influenced by it and in order to act upon it; they are points of contact and of mutual, mixed reality, places of exchange and of communication because they are formed from a knot between the two realities.[30]

The political quality of border mediascapes is determined by the characteristics of each assemblage, described by Simondon as "the reality of the objective world" and "human reality." Technologies, whether old or new, hot or cold, have the capacity to modulate distances and nurture the space of transit, fostering reciprocity between the two shores. When this relationship is absent, boundaries become imbalanced, leading to discrimination and subordination for those who stand on the outer side of the border.

Four Glances in One

Fire at Sea persistently reframes border-setting devices, developing an intermedial inquiry that addresses the spatial and geographical element as much as the human ones. Yet, one of the

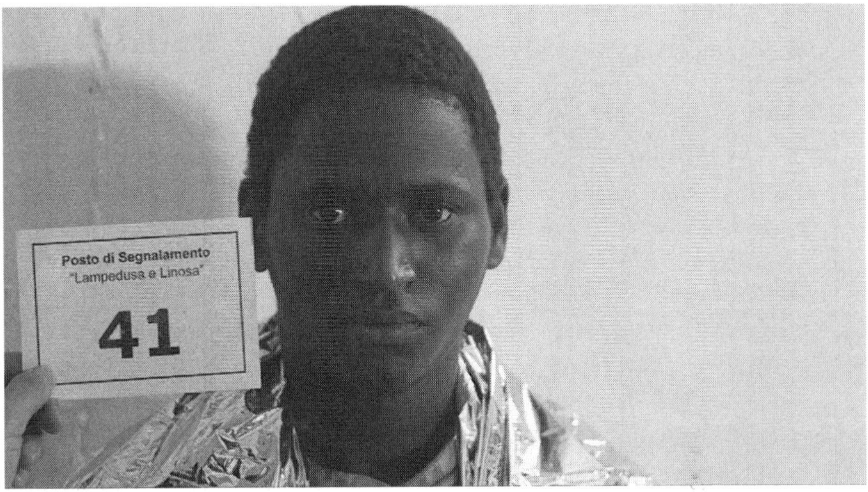

Figure 7. A figure framed frontally, as in a mug shot, invites reflection on the multifaceted functions and meanings of the human face in Western visual culture. Still from *Fire at Sea* (2016).

most impressive scenes in the film is shot face-to-face and with backs to the wall. The migrants have disembarked. Now, they must be searched and registered to be placed at the Contrada Imbriacola hotspot: a central yet isolated facility, operational before 2015 as an Identification and Expulsion Center (CIE) and featured in films produced by the Archivio delle Memorie Migranti (AMM), such as Mario Badagliacca's *Grooving Lampedusa* (2012) and Zakaria Mohamed Ali's *To Whom It May Concern* (2013).[31]

Rosi's camera is set up only a few feet away from a migrant wrapped in an isothermal blanket, whose eyes stare directly into the camera (Figure 7). The framing resembles a mug shot, pointing indexically to a specific identity: "This is subject number 41 of the Lampedusa and Linosa Signaling Post." However, when this kind of shot is introduced into Rosi's exploration of the border mediascape, it inevitably acquires a critical and self-critical function. Within this documentary, the simple photographic exposure of this migrant's body is transformed into a "double exposure," as Mieke Bal describes it: "a strategy for examining the ideological, epistemological, and representational implications of dominating modes of vision."[32] This double exposure alerts us to the fact that the frame contains at least four distinct images—each corresponding to different modes of objectifying the body and face, and thus to four different social and political functions of the portrait.[33]

The identification card next to the migrant's face underscores that this image is first and foremost a mug shot. It conforms to the conventions of this specific type of photographic portrait, which were established in the West starting in the mid-nineteenth century to identify individuals arrested and processed by law enforcement. This visual representation and interpretation also enabled the photographic classification of deviant citizens, as seen in the *portrait parlé* created by the French prefectural official Alphonse Bertillon.[34] The effort to harness photography for police work culminated in Cesare Lombroso's works, which juxtaposed photographs and drawings to make explicit the monstrous appearance of certain faces to identify their potential criminality.[35] Once cataloged and entered into registers or atlases, rarity—physiognomic anomaly—was used as a sign of social and political deviance. This notion of the photographic representation of the human face leads us to the past, but it also brings us back to a present characterized by the intrusiveness of retinal analysis and facial identification technologies. These devices claim to detect individual features in the form of data and process them in detail using digital calculation tools. This is what has been defined as "our biometric future,"[36] when control technologies no longer require a geographical space to implant barriers, because they identify their surface of action in the body and the face. If photography can be counted among the "hot media," we are now at the edge of the cold zone, where the recognition function tends to give way to the identification or detection function.

This quick, simple framing of a migrant in Rosi's film introduces a series of images that evoke other iconographic traditions and other rhetorics of the gaze. What first comes to mind are the communications of humanitarian organizations, which often depict an underprivileged individual looking directly into the camera to bridge the gap between the few physically present on-site who can assist the needy, and the many living far away in comfortable conditions who can only help indirectly by sending money. These campaigns aim to visually remediate and, in a sense, trivialize Levinas's moral theory based on the notion of "face," understood as a form of recognition of the Other, whose "interpellation" is expressed as much by misery, precariousness, and nudity as it is by the eyes. As Levinas writes, "The face has turned to me—and this is its very nudity. . . . This gaze that supplicates and demands, that can supplicate only because it demands, deprived of everything because entitled to everything, and which one recognizes in giving . . . this gaze is precisely the epiphany of the face as a face."[37] We move from Levinas's concept of the face-to-face as the image of morality to its rhetorical simulation in contemporary media discourse. Although Rosi's film acknowledges this trend in recent humanitarian communications, it suggests a way to overcome it, by presenting visual alternatives for an empathic and political perspective. As discussed in previous sections, the rhetoric of compassion is replaced by an observational stance, aiming to understand the mechanisms governing borders. Here, the medium of photography reclaims the idea of heat, though on closer inspection it reveals a humanitarian rhetoric of heat that simulates a closeness between viewers and those in precarious conditions.[38]

A third series of images evoked by this close-up of the migrant involves one of the cornerstones of Western art: the portrait, the idea of representing an individual subject, usually in a frontal position. Portraiture, as a pictorial and sculptural genre, has been practiced in various forms for millennia and has experienced a revival since the Renaissance: first with men of power, then merchants, followed by female aristocrats, and eventually ordinary people. Portraiture aims to represent individuals through their somatic features and the objects that define their place within the space of public recognition, respecting the subject's appearance while also questioning their habitus and status.[39] A portrait serves as the point of contact between individual appearance and social recognition. Humanitarian communications often reduce the face to a compassionate grimace with the look-to-the-camera pose, while anthropometry transforms it into a diagram, turning the individual into a machine-readable scheme. In contrast, the iconographic tradition of the portrait maintains the representation of somatic features, ensuring their legibility and recognizability in a space that is perceptive, public, and political. According to Jean-Luc Nancy, "With the portrait—with its modes, its manners, its eclipses, and its ruins—what is being played out is the fate of the figure in general: the fate of representations, of fiction, therefore of presence and of truth; of the face, of presence and absence; of the other, its proximity and its distance. In the portrait, what is being distinctly retraced, withdrawn, and replayed right before our eyes is the very possibility of our being present."[40] Photography regains its temperature here, in its ability to represent and participate in the construction of a hot media environment—a space made up of reciprocal gazes, encounters, and recognition.

Even more radically, the framing of the man wrapped in the isothermic blanket in Rosi's film engages critically with the history of cinema and the look-to-the-camera—a narrative and rhetorical form that began in a sense with Edwin S. Porter's *Great Train Robbery* (1903) and continues to this day.[41] The look-to-the-camera in *Fire at Sea* should not be seen as a "movie stunt," an effective propaganda solution, or a naive attempt to break the diegetic screen and connect with the external spectator. It is intended rather as a form of interweaving and superimposition of the various functions the portrait assumes in visual culture—a space for critical reflection on these functions, on their aesthetic, ethical, and political limits, and an opportunity to reflect on the circularity and reciprocity of the gaze within social space.

We began this chapter by questioning the relationship between media and forms of recognition. We explored the operational modes of hot and cold media, identifying them as two distinct regimes of contemporary borders. We emphasized moments of thermal instability, which serve as forms of integration between different perceptual regimes, enriching intersubjective practices and forms of recognition. *Fire at Sea*'s look-to-the-camera can be interpreted as a critical evocation of visual forms rooted in portraiture, prompting us to reflect on the contemporary success of anthropometry. It also realizes the aesthetics and ethics of the gaze as theorized by the French critic Serge Daney, who described cinema as a medium capable of teaching "me to ceaselessly touch—with the gaze—that distance between myself and the place where the other begins."[42] This close-up thus acts as a perturbation of the border's temperature: shifting from the coldness of the migrant registration process to the warmth of perceptual recognition and to the look-to-the-camera, revealing the image's ability to touch and attempt to touch us.

CHAPTER 2

OPERATIONAL FRONTIERS

From Above and Below

While I was writing these pages, a wooden boat carrying more than 150 people of Iranian, Pakistani, Afghan, and other descent ran aground in a shoal a few hundred meters from the beaches of Cutro, in Calabria, Italy, on the Ionian Sea. It happened on the night of February 25–26, 2023. Local fishermen were the first rescuers on the scene. Later, some volunteers and carabinieri tried to rescue survivors and began hauling from the water the lifeless bodies that had been pushed toward the shore. According to the latest report from the Crotone Prefecture, there have been ninety-four victims, including thirty-four minors.

European migration policies have no memory: this is neither the first nor the largest massacre of migrants in the Mediterranean, and the traces of past events—whether physical, psychological, or social—are continuously removed and sunk.[1] In Italy, political debate on the topic assumes stances that are as caricatured as they are tragically impactful on reality: from the idea of making videos to persuade departing migrants not to take the voyage to the statement that human traffickers will be hunted down "all over the terraqueous globe."[2] The news focus on responsibilities, on the work of Frontex (the European Border and Coast Guard Agency, to which border control functions are delegated), and on the exchange of information between the competent authorities in the stretch of sea where the tragedy occurred. In a dark area at the center of this debate one finds the technologies that monitor and govern borders, the media network through which nations—in this case, from Italy to Libya—distribute and shrug off rescue and reception responsibilities. How is it possible, many people wonder, to drown two hundred meters off the coast, in an area where every inch of the sea is monitored? In the case of the Cutro shipwreck, what prevented the EU agency Frontex from communicating the exact location of the boat to the military authorities in a timely manner? Why was the search for the boat taken over by the Guardia di Finanza and not by the Italian Coast Guard, which has more effective means in rough seas? And how is one to interpret the recordings of the phone calls in which the NGO Sea Watch questioned the Italian and Libyan coast guards during the twenty-four hours before the shipwreck, without getting any clear response from the national authorities?[3]

This chapter seeks to come to terms with the Mediterranean frontiers and their operational character. I prefer to use the term "frontier" here instead of "border." As we will see in the next few pages, the notion of "operational frontier" shares at least some common territory with that of "border mediascape," of which it defines a strategic component in the hands of states and control authorities. At the heart of this reflection—in the third section of this chapter—I give an account of some of the most interesting projects to appear in academic and public debate in recent years: the counter-investigative work conducted by Forensic Architecture (FA), founded in 2010 at Goldsmiths, University of London. Underlying their project is the idea of bringing multidisciplinary skills and technologies together to investigate cases of human rights violations, with and on behalf of communities affected by political violence, NGOs, international prosecutors, environmental justice groups, and media practitioners.[4] FA's starting assumption is simple: if states and some international authorities exercise functions of territorial and population control by means of specific technologies (a forensic gaze), then we must have forms of counter-vigilance that are free to point the finger at those same states and authorities, for the protection of citizens anywhere in the world. Based on this assumption, the research center has created its own notion, originally proposed by Allan Sekula, of "counter-forensics."[5] As a case study, I will focus particularly on a documentary produced by the FA branch called Forensic Oceanography (FO), funded by Charles Heller and Lorenzo Pezzani. *Liquid Traces* (2014), made by Heller and Pezzani, reconstructs the events of a boat adrift at the heart of the Mediterranean Sea, under the full gaze of the control authorities. In the fourth section I focus on the countershot of the operational frontiers, images made by migrants themselves during their journey. The case study for this section is the film *Purple Sea* (*Das Purpurmeer,* 2020), shot with a waterproof wide-angle-lens camera by Amel Alzakout and re-conceived as a film with Khaled Abdulwahed. The fifth section then turns to *Asmat—Names in Memory of All the Victims of the Sea* (2015) by Dagmawi Yimer, a poignant reflection using words and images to free from anonymity those who lost their lives while attempting to cross the Mediterranean in makeshift vessels. This section of the book also examines the constituent nature of the movements and gestures of those who have faced and are facing the hardships of migration, by which I mean their ability to produce a world to come.

But, before all this, we must take a step back. To enhance the potential of a counter-investigative gaze, especially its idea that images and technologies are "operational" in character, we must first reflect on its aesthetic and epistemic grounds. In the next section, I therefore discuss two concepts—"operational images" and "phantom shot"—originally proposed by the filmmaker, author, and media theorist Harun Farocki, known for his work exploring the relationship between war, capitalism, and technology. Through films and video installations, he critically analyzed the power of images and their function in systems of surveillance. This path deepens the notion of "trace," illustrating how audiovisual language can gather and share traces in public discourse, making the notions of evidence and obscurity work together.

Farocki Point

Forensic Architecture founder Eyal Weizman has spoken on several occasions about his relationship with Harun Farocki during the project's launch phase. In the opening note of the book *Forensic Architecture: Violence at the Threshold of Detectability,* Weizman mentions Farocki as a master filmmaker who was inspired in part by the work of FA: "An earlier version of this essay was published as an introduction to *Forensis: The Architecture of Public Truth* (Berlin: Sternberg Press, 2014), and was the basis for a film that Harun Farocki planned to make using other elements from *Forensis* shortly before his death. This essay is thus dedicated to his memory."[6] In a conversation published in 2016, Yve-Alain Bois remarked to Weizman that many images and videos produced by FA "are similar to Harun Farocki's, and this makes me wonder if one can speak of a 'forensic style.'" Weizman responded with an expression of mutual esteem and interest for the filmmaker: "Farocki's work on machine vision and operative images opened up the sensibility within which we operate. After the *Forensis* exhibition appeared in Berlin, he also got interested in our work and started working on a film on it just a few months before he died."[7] This last point, the description of their meeting and Farocki's film project focusing on FA, is further developed in the first pages of *Investigative Aesthetics,* by Matthew Fuller and Weizman.[8] These statements make explicit a connection that one might take for granted—in the sense of being inevitable. However, beneath any elective affinity lie the epistemic and aesthetic connections between the academic and investigative projects at Goldsmiths and the independent research of the artist and filmmaker. The next few pages present two concepts developed by Farocki that are central to contemporary debates: "operational image" and "phantom shot." The goal of this analysis is to return to FA projects on the Mediterranean border through the framework of film history and theory.

During the latter part of his life, Farocki developed the notion of the operational image *(operative Bilder).* The concept can be seen at work implicitly in multimedia installations such as *Prison Images* (*Gefängnisbilder,* 2000), *War at a Distance* (*Erkennen und Verfolgen,* 2003), and *Counter-Music* (*Gegen-Musik,* 2004) and is found explicitly in *Eye/Machine I–III* (*Auge/Maschine I–III,* 2000–2003).[9] Although Farocki did not provide a clear-cut definition of the operational image, he suggested that it could be identified through military technologies and by investigating their applications and transformations in various domains of civilian life:

> The automatic eye has memorized a handful of filters, through which it scans the images from the real world. These image-processing apparatuses work with a clumsiness reminiscent of robot arms undertaking a new task. Every movement is

> divided into sections, pausing after each partial movement. This may be precise, but without any of the elegance, which might be acquired through habit. Just as mechanical robots initially took workers in the factory as their model, shortly afterwards surpassing and displacing them, so the sensory devices are meant to replace the work of the human eye. Beginning with my first work on this topic *Auge/Maschine [Eye/Machine]*, 2001, I have called such images that are not made to entertain or to inform "operative images." Images that are not simply meant to reproduce something, but instead are part of the operation.[10]

Farocki's comments serve as a starting point to highlight three crucial aspects. First, the idea of the operational image reflects a shift toward conceiving images as procedural or algorithmic tools—tools that can act on behalf of humans and be either beneficial or detrimental to them—heralding the rise of artificial intelligence, machine vision and other technological and artistic trends.[11] This idea refers to technologies and images no longer designed primarily for human vision, to provide aesthetic pleasure or to serve in an exchange of gazes. By way of confirmation, in a note in the introduction to *Forensic Architecture,* Weizman himself echoes Farocki, describing the operational image as "automatically produced by machines for machines transferable as data without ever being converted into anything recognizable by humans as a representation of the visual field."[12] In a similar vein, in a book entirely focused on the Farockian idea of the operational image, Jussi Parikka investigates the relationship between "visuality" and "invisuality." He identifies these as the aesthetic and epistemic cornerstones of a new technological regime, defined more by what images and media do than by what they represent or show to viewers.[13]

A second aspect of Farocki's thought is that these images do not merely represent or simulate a past, present, or future field of reality; rather, they actively influence the field. Just think of "smart bombs," a technological military device designed to destroy whatever it frames. In this sense, the operational image goes beyond both representation and simulation, establishing itself as a protocol that influences the related field of reality and shapes our understanding of it.[14] Here, the image does not merely document something external but can trigger it or, at the very least, be part of an events-based dynamic. Consequently, when the image is considered in terms of its operational character, it cannot be regarded as an eyewitness account of something external or as anything other than itself. Instead, the image is now linked and complicit with what it frames, constituting a logistic juncture for the event.[15] As I will show, these images programmatically negate the traditional documentary function by undermining any spectatorial conception that relies on an idea of representation as a direct visual recognition of actual events. At the same time, their witnessing function can be regenerated, by understanding their operational logic and connection to the field of reality.[16]

A third aspect worth mentioning briefly is the potential relationship between Farocki's notion of *operative Bilder* and Simondon's techno-aesthetics, which I introduced earlier in this book. According to Simondon, media are shaped by and in turn create environments that are both technological and geographic—what he calls a *milieu associé*.[17] Similarly, operational images take this paradigm to extremes and misrepresent its intended meaning. It seems plausible that the operationality of image and media imposes its logic on the targeted territory or environment, unidirectionally altering or sharpening its characteristic features. Put simply, we might say that the more operational technologies tend toward the environment—by setting their sights on it—the more the environment will be shaped by their program. Here, control is the sole purpose for which technological and military means are utilized. This results in their paradoxical nature: as illustrated by Farocki's military examples, at least, the operational image's associated environment is often one that has been destroyed or deeply compromised. Compared to Simondon's formulation, the broken element here is the relationship of reciprocity between the technical component and the physical space, a rupture that also carries significant social and political repercussions. This form of control over territory, social structures, and, more broadly, forms of life aligns with what he describes as a merely *stable* system, as opposed to a *metastable* system that is both balanced and open to becoming: "In all domains, the most stable state is a state of death, i.e. a degraded state starting from which no transformation is possible without the intervention of an external energy to the degraded system."[18] Beyond the idea of destruction, the claim to stabilize large geographical areas through widespread forms of control is evident in the management of contemporary borders. These areas are not environments of destruction but vast areas of monitoring and strategic assessment, or, in the words of Sandro Mezzadra and Brett Neilson, areas governed by an "operational logic."[19]

The second Farockian concept I wish to present is the "phantom shot," also developed in the context of military imaging. This is where humans disappear from the field and are replaced by macro targets, such as military bases or factories. Farocki claims that this notion first emerged in the United States, beginning in the 1920s, to describe "shots filmed from a position normally not taken by a person . . . shots, for instance, from a camera positioned under a train track."[20] He draws once more on military examples:

> Images from the point of view of a person are called *subjectives*. We can therefore regard the shot from the perspective of a bomb as a phantom subjective. The shots taken from the camera that crashes into its target, that is, from a suicide camera, cling to the memory. . . . They appeared together with the word "intelligent weapons," connecting a rather glib idea of intelligence together with an equally glib idea of subjectivity.[21]

Mediation no longer aligns with the viewer's phenomenological experience but instead occurs as a machinic iteration. Visual mediation is "discorrelated" from the viewer's perceptual and cognitive performance.[22] Once a technological device has been programmed, the operators no longer need to monitor and direct its operations. They can maintain a safe distance from the theater of war, remaining as remote from the target as they are from the weapon or source. To whom do these subjectless gazes belong—perceptually, ethically, politically, and legally? We have already addressed this issue in chapter 1. The phantomization of the viewpoint brings with it the question of responsibility, which tends to be sidestepped. Here, the functions of control, defense, and aggression are no longer linked to human intelligence, conscience, or accountability but are transferred to the "intelligence" and "personality" of the image itself.

"Phantom shot" and "operational image" are closely related concepts that help us reflect on the relationship between the subjectivity and objectivity of vision. Like Paul Virilio, Farocki views the images of the First Gulf War as exemplary cases: the fewer the iconic features these "cold" images have to ensure an event's recognizability, the greater their capacity to assume a pragmatic function in triggering it.[23] The issue is highly relevant in today's media and political regimes, particularly with regard to the dematerialization and proliferation of borders: as the architectural and physical components of frontiers disappear, they increasingly align with operational technologies.

A crucial aspect of Farocki's approach, which would later reappear in FA, is his ability to describe the epochal transformations of the techno-aesthetic regime of the new millennium without adopting an apocalyptic or nihilistic attitude. Understanding how operational images work is essential for developing artistic, political, and forensic projects. Before proceeding to the next sections of this chapter, I must emphasize that investigating and critiquing contemporary images and media requires the willingness to engage with other image and media projects. Although Farocki lacked the digital technologies for detection and processing used by FA, he frequently appropriated images produced for military or corporate control of vast areas—such as *Images of the World and Inscription of War* (*Bilder der Welt und Inschrift des Krieges*, 1988)—or confined zones—from *Workers Leave the Factory* (*Arbeiter verlassen die Fabrik*, 1995) to the previously mentioned *Prison Images*. Through these works, he revealed the action protocols of entities equipped with such technologies.[24] The appropriation of operational images can be interpreted as a gesture of resistance against the new regime of images, but, as has been rightly noted, Farocki's practices are not simple acts of contestation.[25]

Drawing inspiration from a famous California landmark featured in Michelangelo Antonioni's *Zabriskie Point* (1970), I propose the idea of a "Farocki Point" to summarize this section. This is not a generic site for the deflagration of technologies, but a point where the testimonial value of operational images, understood as a trace of their bond with the environment and the event they have produced, can be reappropriated. As I will soon highlight, by starting with Farocki's theoretical and artistic work, we can make operational images speak about the operations they conducted or were designed to conduct, the territories they shaped or destroyed, and the perceptual and epistemic asymmetry that structures them. Transforming an operative image into a form of testimony does not mean limiting oneself to what they document about an external field of reality. To restore their testimonial capacity, we must understand how they operate and learn their language, so to speak, so we can subvert and reveal the procedures they use to impose a certain form on reality—in our case, the borders of Mediterranean Europe.

The Farocki Point can thus be understood as a theoretical and critical site where operational images and phantom shots ultimately reveal their influence on reality, along with their operational protocols and systems of responsibility.

Assembling Traces

Forensic Architecture is a multidisciplinary team of researchers skilled in various technologies, ranging from architectural drawing to video-editing software, data visualization, and meteorology, who work on specific political issues or geographic areas. The Forensic Oceanography center has been very active in audiovisual experimentation.[26] Documentaries produced by FO that explore the Mediterranean border include *Death by Rescue* (2016), *The Seizure of the Iuventa* (2018), and *Sea Watch vs the Libyan Coastguard* (2018). These films have been used in court cases, exhibited in art biennials, and screened in galleries.

Liquid Traces lasts about eighteen minutes and reconstructs the events of the so-called Left-to-Die Boat: a boat that departed Libya in March 2011 with seventy-two people and drifted for two weeks after running out of fuel, under the artificial eyes of the control devices and the indifferent gaze of the institutions that oversee the Mediterranean. As Fuller and Weizman write, "Reconstructing shipwrecks is difficult because, as Lorenzo Pezzani and Charles Heller, the directors of Forensic Oceanography, observe, boats do not leave traces on water. Their response was to hyperaestheticise the sea, to augment the sensorial potential of water with secondary sensors that translate fleeting, erasable traces."[27] The term "hyperaestheticise" should not be viewed negatively, as an avoidable spectacularization of the event, but as a method of processing and visualizing data. This process engages different entities with the goal of obtaining, processing, and displaying information about a given situation. Available data

> are then compared to satellite radar imagery and even OSRs—optical sedimentation recorders—measuring the ocean's carbon sequestration capacity and thus its surface disruption. Speaking to survivors, FO helped them reconstruct their memory at sea, the wind and the chain of events leading to the lethal incidents. . . . Later they established the common platform Watch The Med and associated Alarm Phone, which was used both by migrants and by rescuers to coordinate rescues.[28]

The film frame structuring *Liquid Traces* is divided horizontally into three sections. At the center, a cartographic representation of the Strait of Sicily shows the sea surface depicted with blue undulating graphic strokes, reminiscent of the sky in Vincent van Gogh's painting *Starry Night* (*De sterrennacht,* 1889). On the left, the temporal scanning of the facts is schematized on the map, from one to fifteen days. On the right, at the top, a legend explains the different signs and the map scale. In the lower part, displayed and edited from time to time within the frame, a set of documents scrolls by: interviews with survivors, meteorological data, aerial photographs, satellite images, and official documents (Figure 8). The soundtrack, designed to evoke the perceptual condition of the open sea, integrates a series of electronic sounds that accentuate the presence and action of the control technologies.[29]

From the very first minutes, the maritime zones under NATO control and the demarcation lines of the Maltese and Italian search-and-rescue areas are clearly visible. By georeferencing the different positions at the time of the satellite phone calls and by comparing them with the winds and sea currents of the Mediterranean Sea,

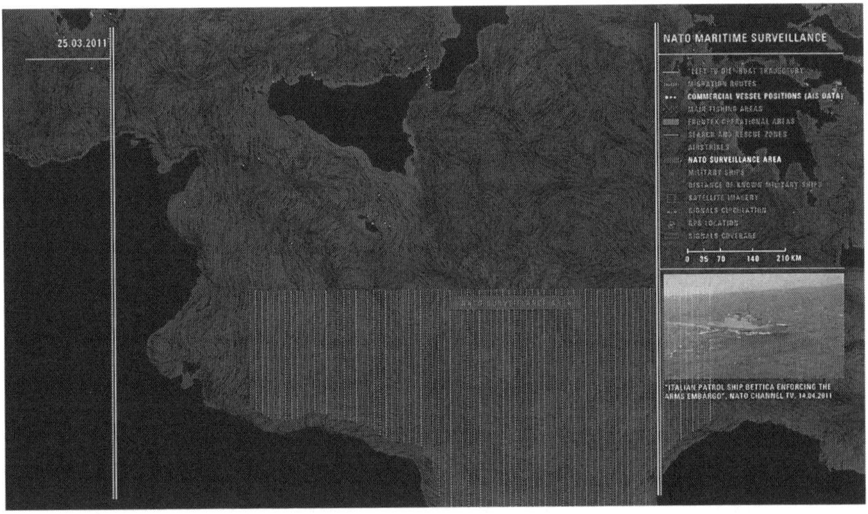

Figure 8. A reconstruction of the route of the Left-to-Die Boat through the Strait of Sicily, using a counter-forensic approach. Still from *Liquid Traces* (2014).

Heller and Pezzani reconstruct the Left-to-Die Boat's route. Their findings reveal politically and legally significant moments while crossing the entire NATO area and entering into Maltese waters—where it was supposed to be rescued—before running out of fuel and drifting.[30] Similarly, in the final part, when recounting the days the boat drifted, the graphic reworking of satellite images shows the presence of numerous large commercial and military vessels that failed to rescue the boat. The film's testimonial effectiveness stems from using the technologies and data that define European borders on the sea and on migrants' bodies as evidence of their operational logic and the competent authorities' failure to rescue the Left-to-Die Boat. The narrative also relies on the audiovisual montage of migrants' SOS recordings overlaid on the Mediterranean map from the zenith viewpoint, highlighting the perceptual state of the migrants during the crossing, the temporality of their experience, and their attempts to connect to the communications device network. This presents viewers with the reconstruction of the facts while also reconnecting the perspectives that structure the visual culture of contemporary borders and migration in the new millennium: the aerial, cartographic view from above and the embodied view from below, grounded in physical, sensorial states. Finally, *Liquid Traces* evokes what the devices of control fail to master in totality: the testimonial source of the natural elements, here reconceived as elemental and climatic media providing information as valuable as it is fragile and liquid.[31] The focus is on wind and water, their speed, expressed as the relationship between space traveled and time spent, and their effect on the dynamics of the Left-to-Die Boat's travel and drift.

The European border mediascape that emerges from Heller and Pezzani's film is clearly shown to be the result of a strategic arrangement. The geography of the environmental media lacks any potential for reciprocity, whether toward those from the southern shore of the Mediterranean or toward the sea and other elements. Fernand Braudel's *longue durée* investigation of the Mediterranean Sea comes to mind, where Braudel writes that the body of water was first conceived as "an obstacle" but later, with the advancement of navigational knowledge and techniques, as "a surface for transport, a useful surface, if not perfect[, where] the ship, the sea route, the well-equipped port, the merchant city are tools at the service of Mediterranean cities, states, and economies—the tools of their exchanges and, consequently, of their wealth."[32] In contrast to the conclusions of the French historian, *Liquid Traces* demonstrates a reversal of this trend. Technologies, once unifying, now divide: national and international control bodies use the lines on the map to chart tracks that turn the open sea into an obstacle for some and a transportation surface for others. This difference elucidates the suggestion I made earlier about the waves of the sea, depicted in *Liquid Traces* as van Gogh's starry sky. While starry nights have guided mariners across open seas around the world and throughout the ages, the lines and points of light found on the cartographic surface now express a network of power relationships.

As the film draws to an end, the voice-over discloses the Left-to-Die Boat's tragic fate:

> For fourteen days, the passengers have slowly drifted across the most heavily surveilled waters on earth. Despite repeated

> contacts, sixty-three passengers were killed because of the reluctance of all actors to rescue them. But nine people survived to tell their stories. By assembling their testimonies with digital traces left behind by events, we were able to map the trajectory of their boat across the liquid geography of the sea: every point and every line drawn on this map seeks to inscribe responsibility in a sea of impunity.

The concluding words of *Liquid Traces* make clear that it is an assemblage of heterogeneous media traces intended to reconstruct and make visible the dynamics of the events in order to determine responsibility for the shipwreck and make the logic of evidence prevail over obscurity. In taking up the notion of "trace," which appears in the film's title and is central to FA's self-narrative, I want to avoid any potential positivism associated with this notion, thus steering clear of any simplistic conception of truth, which has been deconstructed philosophically since at least the second half of the twentieth century. Jacques Derrida's seminal work demonstrated that each trace carries with it a dual absence, referring both to the idea of "origin" and to the wholeness of its meanings.[33] Developing Derrida's thought in a techno-aesthetic direction, Bernard Stiegler explored how technics can either acknowledge or deny the gap between past and present that each trace brings with it. Media can work constructively by recognizing and valuing the gap between origin and present, thereby acknowledging the Derridean concept of *différance*. Conversely, media may attempt to negate this gap, striving to close the distance from the origin. However, in doing so they risk compromising the nature of the trace, reducing time and memory to mechanical repetition and precluding critical reflection.[34] This does not mean giving up on working with traces or the pursuit for a truth that is valid in public discourse and the legal arena. On the contrary, it suggests that working with traces involves continuous aestheticizations or "hyperaestheticizations" that can make various aspects appear or disappear, thereby valuing certain origins and meanings over others.

Concealing aesthetic and technological efforts to reveal traces of a past event and give them a voice does not lend them greater credibility. Quite the opposite: explaining these interventions guarantees the specific testimonial value of the trace, along with its various other meanings and functions. This value should be recognized not only in forensic contexts but also in public discourse, serving as a means to understand the mechanisms of border management and to foster public awareness. My goal here is to underscore the distinctly Farockian quality of Heller and Pezzani's work, characterized by its fusion of cinematographic and forensic aspects. In their work, each montage of images functions as an assemblage, insofar as it calls into question both the mechanical and information technology components and the spatial and environmental aspects. This filmic assemblage of traces effectively serves as an intermedial investigation into the technological and geopolitical arrangements that determined the event in question.

To summarize what we have discussed thus far, *Liquid Traces* investigates the operational nature of frontiers and reflects it back to viewers, problematizing it. The first issue raised by the film is that these geographic areas are monitored continuously by technologies that have largely been delegated the governance function, effectively offloading onto them the responsibilities for "incidental" shipwrecks. The second issue, echoing the three points I discussed regarding *operative Bilder* in the previous section, involves the agency of technologies set up to control the Mediterranean. In the absence of walls or ridges to clearly demarcate Libyan and Italian waters, the cartographic image is projected onto the territory using technologies that sustain the idea of frontiers. According to this understanding of technology and geography, the map actually tends to coincide with the territory.[35] The third issue brings us back to the quality of environments associated with operational frontiers and the complex system of alerts, detections, and information exchanges between competent authorities, facilitating interventions and rescues or, in many cases, due to their tragic absence, leading to acts of deliberate negligence. *Liquid Traces* reveals the absurdity of a shipwreck occurring in a geographical area under continuous monitoring, one of many such incidents. It reconstructs and denounces the reality that contemporary frontiers serve as instruments of biopolitical governance and as mechanisms of what Achille Mbembe termed "necropolitics," where states and supranational bodies allow or cause the death of tens, hundreds, and thousands of migrants by drowning, dismissing these systematic occurrences as "fatalities" due to sea or weather conditions.[36]

The Farocki Point, a theoretical and critical site of practice for filmmakers, seeks to reveal the different points of view that coexist on the same stretch of sea, exposing a plurality of trajectories and travel speeds, and a multiplicity of human and nonhuman actors that affirm the reality of the border. By enabling traces to become visible through montage, documentary cinema inherently possesses a "forensic" quality, evident in both its history and its present. Consequently, in the following sections we will look at other films focused on the Mediterranean frontiers, understood in two senses: as technological and operational borders, and as a liquid environment—a specific experiential condition for those compelled to cross it.

Along the Waterline

In 2020, Forensic Architecture produced the audiovisual project *Shipwreck at the Threshold of Europe, Lesvos, Aegean Sea,* investigating the tragic events of October 28, 2015, when a boat of migrants leaving Turkey and heading to the Greek island of Lesvos sank, killing at least forty-three people.[37] This twenty-three-minute work is based on footage shot by the Syrian artist Amel Alzakout during the shipwreck of the boat in which she was trying to reach Europe. The media document corresponding to the perceptual "from below" experience of the shipwreck is edited together with information from various sensing technologies. The aim of this audiovisual document is to offer a narrative of the events' dynamics and to identify responsibilities, through the frontier management system.

As if to underscore the nexus between investigation and creativity that I highlighted in the preceding sections of this chapter, the images produced by Alzakout included in the FA video can be found in one of the most interesting experimental documentaries on border management and migration: *Purple Sea.* Created by Alzakout together with Khaled Abdulwahed, it was presented at

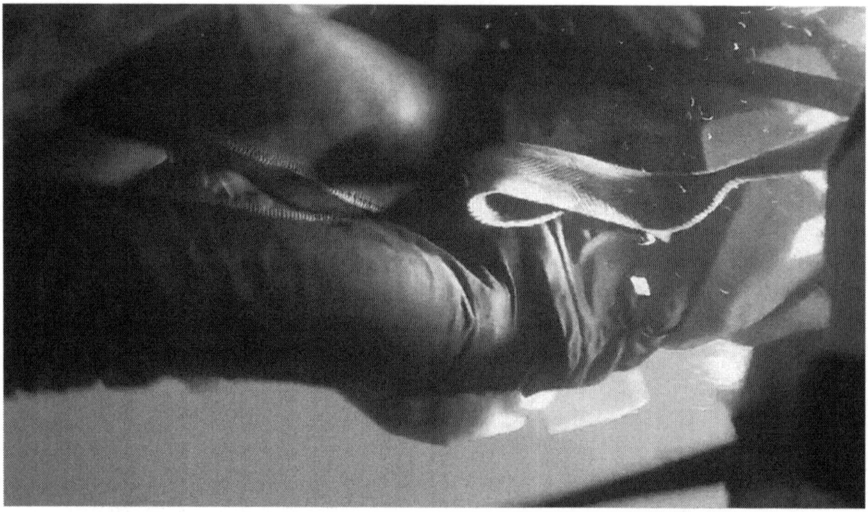

Figure 9. An underwater shot capturing the material condition of the shipwreck. Still from *Purple Sea* (2020).

the Berlin Film Festival in 2020 and has been widely discussed in film studies and by political and social scientists.[38]

Purple Sea is based on images taken with a waterproof, wide-angle-lens video camera. During the shipwreck between Turkey and the island of Lesvos, in a stretch of open sea suddenly crowded with men and women wearing life jackets and hoping to be rescued, Alzakout keeps the camera recording to document what is happening along the waterline. The voice-over, retrofitted to the images, recounts her attempts to apply for a visa to join her partner, codirector Abdulwahed, in Germany.

The film explores how the water element is deliberately shaped into an obstacle for those attempting to reach Europe from certain areas of the planet. The transformation of the sea into a necropolitical element—devoid of communication and transportation grounded in reciprocity—serves as the material foundation for developing an aesthetic and political reflection. For migrants immersed forcibly in the sea, the world appears divided in two parts: those who live safely on dry land and those whose skin color, nationality, or other circumstances condemn them to remain submerged in the cold, while struggling to avoid drowning.

The underwater setting, which lasts throughout the film, starkly highlights the "color line" dividing the "Global North" from the "Global South" or, at the very least, underscores the strategic relationship between the Mediterranean's different shores and the dramatic, paradoxical effects they produce. "The cat takes the plane to Berlin, no visa required," says Alzakout at one point. Her quip succinctly captures the geopolitical regime that compels millions of people mostly from Asian and African nations to undertake perilous journeys to Europe, often organized by traffickers and smugglers, involving emergency vehicles, shipwrecks, and the hope for spectacular open-sea rescues.[39] Despite originating from the war-torn nation of Syria, the filmmaker's account reveals the diverse motivations behind travel and migration. Alzakout's voice bridges the gap between forced migration and voluntary migration, prompting us to question the validity of such a rigid distinction. This aspect has emerged previously in ethnographic research on the experiences and perspectives of migrant women in the Mediterranean context. While many may have fled from war or violence, "some women may say that they came to Europe to join neighbors and friends, to earn a living and escape poverty, to find better job opportunities. This is not exactly new to migration research: for decades, many studies have recognized the mixed motivations, which are sometimes not compatible with the vision of international law."[40]

The montage—the tension between what is seen and what is heard—creates other unexpected effects that critically renew our gaze on migration. In contrast to the tense, agitated circumstances of the shipwreck, the temporality of the images and the narrative seems to dilate while waiting for rescue vehicles to arrive.[41] While the voice-over varies erratically—from recounting her dreams and expressing love for her partner to recalling memories of Syria and describing the sensations of cold—the underwater images are marked by bright, shimmering chromatics (Figure 9). Bodies and objects slow down when immersed in the aquatic environment. What reviewers have termed "stream of consciousness" in the film should be understood as referring not only to the text and voice but also to the images themselves.[42]

Studies on other audiovisual experiments made with so-called action cameras—especially *Leviathan* (2012) by Lucien Castaing-Taylor and Verena Paravel of the Sensory Ethnography Lab at Harvard[43]—reveal that this wide-angle underwater gaze can re-articulate and expand the limits of cinematographic sensibility, transcending the dichotomies of subject and object, perception and sensation.[44] Similarly, the shots in *Purple Sea* are not captured through a viewfinder controlled by an operator: they originate from the camera's direct interaction with the body it is attached to, and the unique inertia of the aquatic environment. The camera movements are guided more by the interaction between bodies and their environment than by a director's gaze.[45] As we have seen, the "operational images" and "phantom shots" that Farocki described consist of a kind of machine takeover of the position traditionally assumed by human beings, a position of perceptual, cognitive, and pragmatic control and dominance. By contrast, the images of *Purple Sea* are distinguished by their ability to dissolve that centrality, whether human or machine. In media theory discussion, water has been spoken of as an "interface" that can separate and connect what is immersed in it.[46] Along the same lines, *Purple Sea*'s camera documents a visible space along with the impersonal movements and, synesthetically, the sensory condition of the bodies immersed in water. As the visual perspective becomes more impersonal, Alzakout's vocal narrative becomes more personal and intimate, questioning the stark separation between subject and environment, human and nonhuman.

In the previous section we saw how images and data from the sea surface can be transformed into an audiovisual narrative and used for forensic purposes. The recording made by Alzakout was essential to the investigation *Shipwreck at the Threshold of Europe, Lesvos, Aegean Sea*. Nonetheless, the same cinematic traces can also assume other expressive functions and possible meanings. A shipwreck is a tragic event that demands witnessing: this objective remains central to Alzakout and Abdulwahed's film. At the same time, the film seems to reflect on and invite us to consider the "liquid traces" of the shipwreck in other ways as well. In addition to their forensic value, these images bear other forms of truth, allowing us to observe and condemn the injustices of technological and political systems while also experiencing affirmative aesthetic and political possibilities. The underwater camera offers an opportunity for a critical view of the technological and epistemic paradigms that govern borderlands under the pretext of forced stabilization. The loss of spatial and temporal orientation also challenges a certain conception of space and time: it exposes the hypocrisy of continuously monitoring a geographic space, conceived and designed with radically asymmetrical structures, under the guise of emergency response and prompt rescue.

Written on the Water

As frontiers become operational and artistic and forensic projects explore their workings and accountability systems, some films document shipwrecks and the aquatic environment. Their goal is to reverse and decentralize the human perspective, fostering respect for the idea of life and its protection. This is the case with *Purple Sea*. Other films express care for those who have lost their lives at sea and the ways European public discourse addresses the migration issue. These include *Asmat—Names in Memory of All the Victims of the Sea* (2015), produced to commemorate the massacre that occurred on October 3, 2013, off the island of Conigli, near Lampedusa.

Asmat, which means "names" in Tigrinyia, is directed by Ethiopian-born Dagmawi Yimer, who arrived in Italy in 2006 and has directed several other films. The tale of the tragic shipwreck unfolds through different expressive forms, alternating underwater images, drawings, footage of a performance taking place a few yards from the shore, and graphic animation. The first part of the film features drawings documenting the shipwreck, accompanied by a female voice-over and the sound of a stringed instrument. First, the voice addresses African politicians, holding them responsible for those forced to flee their home nations. The same voice then turns to European politicians, reminding them of the values and rights their continent is believed to uphold. It then posits that the way migrants are treated serves as a continual test of the civilization they represent and take pride in. Finally, it calls on people of faith to recognize those who arrive from afar—the other—as close, neighboring, and fraternal figures.[47] As the voice

Figure 10. The names of the victims of the October 3, 2013, shipwreck are superimposed over underwater images, turning the sea into a medium for memorial and political inscriptions. Still from *Asmat—Names in Memory of All the Victims of the Sea* (2015).

pronounces these words, we see images of a performance taking place just steps from the shore, poised between above and below the surface.

Asmat then plunges underwater. A series of names stand out in overlay on the sandy seabed as the voice-over calls them out, commemorating them one by one (Figure 10). As the names of those who lost their lives in the October 3, 2013, shipwreck are read out, their original meanings are translated on the screen. In a statement accompanying the film, Yimer himself makes explicit that "The film's images give space to these names without bodies. They are meaningful names although it might be difficult for us to grasp their meaning. It is necessary for us to count them all, name each and every one, to make us aware of how many names lost their bodies on one single day, in the Mediterranean sea."[48]

Along with *Asmat,* other films have also taken on the task of reconstructing shipwrecks and commemorating the victims. Madeleine Leroyer's *#387* (2019), despite its more conventional aesthetic structure, shows the efforts of those who worked to re-establish the identities of the victims of the April 18, 2015, shipwreck off the coast of Libya, where over eight hundred people lost their lives. This is one of the most tragic shipwrecks in the Mediterranean in recent decades. Both *Asmat* and *#387* exhibit and denounce the role of technologies in structuring processes of discrimination and racialization at borders. These films explicitly condemn what we have defined as the strategic configuration of the border mediascape, an attempt to brutally preserve a "White Mediterranean."[49] Within this conception, different media operating in borderlands do not fulfill the function of guaranteeing fundamental rights or protecting the conditions of those in need or willing to travel. Instead, they amplify the securitarian function of borders and ensure the maintenance of established power relations. As noted, the decision to film *Asmat* using underwater and overwater images—depicting the plight of the "drowned" and the "saved"—highlights a structural asymmetry that calls upon everyone, especially those in privileged positions. European and Western citizens only belong to a protective system of citizenship thanks to the "disposition of maintaining the vast majority of the world in a state of non-citizenship and unfreedom."[50]

A thread running through this chapter ties seemingly very distant films together. For traces of an event to be cherished and made to speak, whether implicit or explicit, they need a practice and a form of writing that houses and creatively implements them, which may be audiovisual or of some other kind. The attempt to trace rights violations in the liquid environment of the Mediterranean and to view migrants' sea routes as a form of writing are two sides of the same coin. In both cases, these gestures aim to acknowledge the importance of what happens in border areas. The discovery of injustices perpetrated over the years and the recounting of journeys should be considered decisive elements in the process of political regeneration. As one of the authors of *Liquid Traces* writes in a 2017 text, "the sea is one of the assembly spaces of the migrants' constituent, which defines its modes of communal living through the migrants' own movements. A constituent whose text can be found written directly on the surface of the sea, as an act and without delegation, but which we refuse to read."[51]

CHAPTER 3

AN ARCHAEOLOGY OF THE FORTRESS

Frames

Exterior, night. A human figure, a security guard, opens a series of bolts and walks through a gate, inside a building, and then into a dormitory: "Hello! It's time. Transfer. Chiasso!" The camera follows him in darkness and in full light, from the outside to the inside, until a montage cut brings our view back outside the building. Framed now from bottom to top is the facade, the geometric design of the windows (Figure 11). Thanks to the backlighting, we are able to identify the silhouettes of the people inside the building. Less an establishing shot, meant to inform us about the where and when of the events in question, this is a series of shots, or re-shots, in which men, women, and children intent on praying, washing, or preparing food are shown through the architectural frame of the window. The point of view then returns to the interior, where people appear to move agitatedly, called by men in uniform to hurry down to facilitate their own transfer. Finally, an editing cut shows us something different still: we recognize a few frames taken from the surveillance camera, placed on the threshold of the building—a mechanical eye that monitors and normalizes behavior, which, by following people inside and outside, helps to differentiate spaces and regulate access.

Thus begins *The Fortress* (*La forteresse,* 2008), the main case study of this chapter, through which I reflect on the specific figure of the border as represented by centers in various European countries where migrants are interned, identified, and put on file. The film was directed by Fernand Melgar, a Swiss filmmaker born in Morocco of Spanish descent, and shot at the Federal Asylum

Figure 11. The Federal Asylum Centre in Vallorbe, Switzerland, an institution governed by forms of discipline and control. Still from *The Fortress* (2008).

Centre (FAC) in Vallorbe, Switzerland. This is where dozens of people of all ages, from Togo, Georgia, Kosovo, Colombia, and many other countries, are forced to stay while waiting to learn the outcome of their asylum applications to the Swiss Confederation.[1]

The aim of this opening description is to highlight the conceptual core of the entire film: the importance assumed by the "frame," understood as a mechanism of separation—architectural, social, and political, but also and primarily a media mechanism—that constructs a field of subjects and objects.[2] In the language of filmology, a beginning that foreshadows the entire story thematically and compositionally is called a "predestination plot," an implicit allusion to the narrative process and outcome. But, as I explain in detail in this chapter, Melgar's insistence on the external facade of the building and the prominence assigned to the bodies of the internees, seen through the surveillance camera monitors, constitutes the specific investigative strategy of the film. Therefore, what is shown in the opening sequence does not so much anticipate the ending—the umpteenth transfer of asylum seekers—as it defines the analytical approach of the camera and its ability to observe and understand the functioning of an asylum seeker registration center, one of the most important figures of the border that appears on the contemporary scene.

During the past few years, *The Fortress* has been used repeatedly as a term of comparison for ethnographic inquiries and critical reflections on migratory management.[3] While drawing on this literature, my aim here is to approach it from the perspective of film and media archaeology, taking advantage of cinema's special ability to explore the layered and multifaceted character of borders.[4] After this introduction, the second section of this chapter delves into the idea of "Fortress Europe," an idea that connects contemporary management structures of migratory phenomena to the geopolitics of Europe during the first half of the twentieth century. This study on *The Fortress,* along with regular references to Melgar's other films on migration and the right to asylum—*Special Flight* (*Vol spécial,* 2011), *The Shelter* (*L'abri,* 2014), and *The World Is Like That* (*Le monde est comme ça,* 2013)—suggests that viewing FACs and other, similar facilities from an archaeological perspective helps to bring out the complexity of these institutions.

My analysis of sequences from these films further leads to the idea of "border mediascaping," understood as a media and political practice used in the management of perimeters and hybrid zones that intertwines notions of sovereignty and governmentality. Assuming these asylum processing centers are situated both inside and outside the nation-state system, the third section underlines the ritual and theatrical character of the protocols and discursive forms that characterize such spaces. Out of this emerge the practices through which the subjectivity of migrant men and women is reconceived—or rather, reframed—as the position of the "asylum seeker" and becomes their only possible form of recognition. In treating the border as a space of mandatory adaptation to a set of discursive, visual, and narrative patterns, I highlight the presence of religious organizations and figures that offer comfort and exercise a moral function over individuals waiting to have their asylum applications processed. Points of overlap between the institutional discourse, which purports to be secular, and the religious discourse become evident, providing feedback for studies on the forms of assistance and management of migrants as forms of secularization that have developed over the past few years. The fourth section returns to Melgar's documentary gaze by proposing a model for his filmmaking in the observational documentary tradition, a tradition that has always been interested in investigating the workings of institutional bodies.

The Dialectics of Times and Spaces

When we consider why a particular title was chosen, we necessarily embark on a journey of discovery into a film's unspoken and unseen analytical and critical insights, along with its related historical, geographical, and political issues. The idea of "Fortress Europe" has returned with varying frequency in the public discourse of the new millennium, expressing both the idea of inaccessibility (for those on the outside) and the claim for protection (for those on the inside). The expression has also been used in the battle for human rights and to denounce the systematic violence to which migrants are subjected in contemporary Europe. But resorting to such an expression means to employ a powerful architectural and geopolitical metaphor that establishes a dialectic, though not an analogy, between the present time and the darkest moments of the twentieth century. This is because it refers explicitly to the German *Festung Europa,* used to indicate the defense system of continental Europe under the dominance of Nazi Germany.

In his book *Bunker Archeology,* Paul Virilio explores military architectures, particularly those built by Nazi Germany during World War II. As always in Virilio's research, the case studies become the starting point for developing a reflection at the crossroads of different disciplines and interests. In particular, the book focuses on three fundamental aspects of Fortress Europe that are essential for reflecting on the use of this metaphor in the contemporary context: its architectural configuration, its evolution into a system of remote surveillance, and its symbolic power in shaping behaviors, identities, and national sentiment.

The first aspect of Virilio's thought relates to the territorial dislocation of Fortress Europe, which was able to extend over geographical space through interconnected buildings—not exclusively near political borders but in any part of the territory. As

Virilio states, "The ramparts that, in preceding centuries, moved from the limits of the city to the limits of the nation-state moved once again to the limits of emergent land. The Fortress Europe is the sign of that moment in history when the surface of the world exposed itself to aggression."[5] The second aspect concerns the fact that the Fortress expressed the presence of physical constructions installed on the territory as well as the progressive use of media technologies that guarded the geographic and political space at a distance and facilitated timely intervention:

> What seems most significant in the defensive movement is the progressive disappearance of surface equipment, the fantastic development of alert systems, the electronic arsenal of what were already called "invisible arms." . . . In fact, most of the means for acoustic detection had been created during the First World War, but optical telemetering, radiophony, and radar were further improved during the Second World War.[6]

A third aspect of Fortress Europe in Virilio's work thus coincides with the symbolic efficacy it exerted on the subjects living and working within the frontier line as well as inside and outside the fronts. The Fortress magnified the principle of the "security" and "sacredness" of national territories; in doing so, it also imposed a behavior on those employed to manage it, on those it protected, and on those it threatened. In other words, the system of territorial garrison structures constituted a ceremonial strategy for exerting an effect of reassurance and threat. Virilio describes another facet of this aspect at the beginning of the chapter on Fortress Europe: "War is at once a summary and a museum . . . its own. War is at once prospective and retrospective; fortifications aim not only to conserve power but also to conserve all combat techniques."[7] Later, he again underlines that the "sociopolitical role of the enceinte in the establishment of communal or national sentiment is too often forgotten."[8]

Just as Virilio's archaeological approach has served to investigate and problematize the use of the medieval image of a fortress when speaking about military structures in Europe in the 1940s, a different kind of archaeology must be developed to arrive at a contemporary idea of the fortress. The first two characteristics of

Fortress Europe—its physical installation throughout the continent and the large geographical scale over which its technology is articulated—also emerge with particular force from Melgar's investigation. Here, the borderscape consists of continuous assemblages between different kinds of technologies. Although the film shot in the Vallorbe FAC is titled *The Fortress,* it expresses a conception that is anything but static. If the architecture of internment justifies the label of a "disciplinary" system, then the presence of media and protocols by which the living spaces and schedules of migrants are managed, with or without direct contact, legitimates the idea of "control," as defined in the context of French philosophy.

As is well-known, Michel Foucault defined *discipline* as a "technology of power" established in the modern age, whose aim is to govern subjects through forms of visibility and containment, with or without the use of physical violence. "Discipline," writes Foucault, "presupposes a mechanism that coerces by means of observation; an apparatus in which the techniques that make it possible to see induce [*sic*] effects of power, and in which, conversely, the means of coercion make those on whom they are applied clearly visible."[9] Great importance is given to spatial organization and architecture, defined in the name of its capacity to "operate to transform individuals: to act on those it shelters, to provide a hold on their conduct, to carry the effects of power right to them, to make it possible to know them, to alter them. Stones can make people docile and knowable."[10] The paradigm of *control,* on the other hand, was conceived by Gilles Deleuze as a "new generation" technology of power, capable of being exercised on a large scale and with a smaller outflow of force. As Deleuze stresses, Foucault situated disciplinary societies between the seventeenth and the nineteenth centuries; however, to understand our contemporary scene we must give greater weight to how the control is implemented: "The old sovereign societies worked with simple machines, levers, pulleys, clocks; but recent disciplinary societies were equipped with thermodynamic machines . . . control societies function with a third generation of machines, with information technology and computers."[11]

As in different sequences of the film, the entry and exit of

Figure 12. Monitoring of the space around the Federal Asylum Centre. Still from *The Fortress* (2008).

asylum seekers from the FAC is controlled through images from closed-circuit television cameras. In some cases, Melgar frames the control monitors in a semi-subjective shot, by including the official who is shadowing the migrants (Figure 12). In other instances the control monitor is framed full-screen, without any control personnel shown in the frame. As in previous chapters, here too technological control offers the ability to activate mechanisms for managing a given environment at distance. Even a simple surveillance camera has the power to condition the behaviors of people who are aware they are being monitored.

Once inside the facility, Melgar's camera shows the organization of the FAC's architectural space and its system of rules, the standard procedures and forms of interaction between the migrants and the personnel who provide assistance and perform moral, security, and legal functions. Rather than oppose each other or alternate in a chronological pattern, discipline and control intertwine in the concrete functioning of various management protocols.[12] On the one hand, a global framework formally obligated to protect human rights requires the development of technologies of power that can capture and manage spaces and bodies, schedule their daily activities, and follow their movements, by insinuating themselves into their psychological and biological lives. On the other hand, the construction of walls and the architectural structures of internment remains a fundamental strategy even in contemporary institutions, as Melgar's subsequent film *Special Flight* shows through the recurrence of physical coercion.

To take up an issue that emerged in chapter 1, border facilities such as the one shown in Melgar's film, or the "hotspots" deployed on the continental borders of Europe,[13] result from a continuous interweaving of what I propose to call "hot media environment" (involving strong perceptual and emotional engagement with the subjects) and "cold media environment" (remotely controlled, in which interactions between subjects are delegated to technological tools).[14] In this sense, every *hotspot* is always, simultaneously, also a *coldspot*—that is, a sensorial space characterized by hierarchical forms of contact and interaction assisted to varying degrees by technology.

Asylum seekers are interned in a facility that provides a range of amenities, such as dormitories, a canteen, a prayer room, a sports field, and so forth; they are also allowed to go in and out of the facility, although these exits and entries are subject to control. But the city life located just around the corner remains off-screen: the camera's focus is always on the inside of the FAC and on the threshold space, both physical and digital, between inside and outside. As has been noted, in this "representation of the Swiss asylum system, which includes no spoken commentary, it is above all nature that suggests that something is wrong. The facility is surrounded by snow-covered mountains; it is cold, and it rains."[15] Rather than conceiving of the FAC as a space closed or open to the outside world, Melgar underscores the fact that it is at once rooted in a specific geographic location (the Alpine border) and connected at a distance with other facilities (such as the one to which asylum seekers are transferred in the film or where they will be deported to in their home countries) that are part of the border infrastructure.[16] What is missing, then, is the contextual environment of the FAC, the horizon of proximity in which civic life takes place in the town of Vallorbe, in the Swiss Federation, and on the European continent. In other words, the structure of the FAC constitutes an environment folded in on itself, it fits within the Alpine geographic environment in a way that exploits and strengthens the impervious nature and difficult routes that characterize such areas to disadvantage asylum seekers. The facility creates a milieu of segregation around itself, or turns the mountain ridge into a frontier. Here we are faced with an interesting actualization of the "color line" device described in the introduction. The eminently biopolitical character of the facility emerges precisely from this condition of geographical separation: a range of personal services and comforts are provided to asylum seekers, but this does not involve their integration into the system of social life or citizenship.[17]

Over the past few years, scholars in philosophy, law, and geography have engaged in a critical return to questions raised in Carl Schmitt's concept of *Nomos* (spatial order).[18] This approach has emphasized an expansion-oriented conception of borders, rather than one primarily concerned with defense or containment. What has thus emerged is the relationship between the design of European national frontiers in modern and contemporary times and how the lines of colonial expansion were projected outward.[19] This has brought into focus the appropriative character of geography, whose outlines are sharpened in the context of global exploration and colonial expansion. *The Fortress* and Melgar's later works investigate and show us a completely new context than the one in which the concept of Fortress Europe and the geopolitical notions proposed by Schmitt emerged. Yet these films also show us that certain geopolitical designs continue to be imposed on territories and bodies. Throughout Melgar's films we observe the techniques and protocols by which the spatial order of the frontier continues to govern the lives of migrants, creating dynamics of integration or rejection in distant countries. What appears is not only the national frontier but also the specific process I am calling "border mediascaping": the technological establishment and preservation of "exceptional" spaces that do not coincide with the systems of guarantees offered by the state to its citizens but are governed rather through the overlapping of sovereignty and governmentality. Echoing the FAC's peculiar form of isolation mentioned earlier, it is as if border mediascaping practices

Figure 13. An airplane in flight, viewed through the bars of a grate, illustrating the spatial and functional continuity across facilities for migrant containment, rejection, and repatriation. Still from *Special Flight* (2011).

were intended to ensure that these identification facilities remain separate from the city center, while nevertheless guaranteeing their connection with similar facilities and other governmental apparatuses.[20]

Films shot in borderlands show the heterogeneity of cultural practices and techniques that define these spaces as the point of access of people who originate almost exclusively from what was once called the "Third World" and is now referred to as the "Global South." Borders appear as specific areas where information from different continents is accumulated; they also appear as places of implementation of decisions, where it is determined who can be integrated into the national community and who must be expelled to their country of origin—almost always a former colony of a European state. For this reason, the two environments of the prison and the airplane, which are profoundly different, if not opposite, in terms of motion and function, can be shown as a single continuum designed for the containment, rejection, and repatriation of migrants. In this case I am referring specifically to the shot in *Special Flight* in which an airplane flying overhead is filmed from inside the cell into which migrants awaiting extradition have been forced (Figure 13).

The infrastructural, technological, and geopolitical articulation of the border is the main theme of all the films that Melgar dedicates to the management of migratory phenomena: *The Fortress* investigates the Vallorbe FAC; *Special Flight* focuses on the Frambois administrative detention facility in Geneva; and *The Shelter* shows Lausanne's emergency accommodation centers, primarily intended for European citizens. The relationship between these facilities and the nations from which asylum seekers originate is addressed explicitly in *The World Is Like That,* made by Melgar for Swiss television. This film follows the protagonists of *Special Flight* after they have been deported to Kosovo, Senegal, Gambia, and Cameroon. Because of the rejection these individuals experienced in Europe, they will be subjected once again to the dismissal of their rights. The process comes full circle.

The fortress is not so much a wall or a sharp line between two states, but a network of buildings, legal mechanisms, and media devices connecting facilities in different places, even on an intercontinental scale. Those who fail to obtain some form of recognition as a gateway, those who enter the round of transfers from one facility to another, are subjected to continuous disenfranchisement. Here, the fortress metaphor appears in all its violence, serving as a welding point and bridge between past and present.

(Un)doing the Refugee

After working on the first two levels, we turn now to the third level suggested in Virilio's exploration of Fortress Europe: the eminently symbolic and performative function of border management structures. In what sense can an FAC be regarded as "a museum of itself," or as a theatrical space that assigns a "role" and a "part" to the people inside it?

For about an hour and a half, Melgar's camera moves through the FAC: it records the facility director's meetings with the staff, the daily actions of the asylum seekers, their moments of bewilderment, and their interactions with the authorities and security officers. This effortless ability to navigate spaces and build trust—without creating overt complicity—undoubtedly stems from the film director's long-standing acquaintance with the institution and its employees.[21] Just past the halfway point of the film, the camera shows the activities of a clergyman, who is telling a group of children the story of the forty days Jesus spent in the desert resisting the devil's temptations (Matthew 4:1–4). Later, during the collective reading of the sacred texts, he makes an invocation to God: "You are my refuge and my fortress, my God in whom I trust" (Psalm 91:2). After this quotation from the psalm—which also recalls the title of the film—we witness a long face-to-face meeting between the priest and a young Somali migrant. The latter acts out the stages of his journey as he recounts the reasons for his escape from his homeland and the many challenges he has faced. Questioned by the priest, with the assistance of an interpreter, he dwells on the most painful details and on the atrocious aspects of his experience. He describes the gunshot wounds he received in Somalia and shows his scars. He then focuses on his month-long journey on foot through the desert and his voyage across the Mediterranean aboard an eight-meter pirogue. He even mentions cannibalism onboard after ten days adrift.

Despite the priest's sustained tone of compassion and absolution, the film montage isolates the two figures by means of the shot/countershot technique. The space is split in two to enhance the confessional character of the episode. Through this compositional choice, the film creates a peculiar spatial quality that explicitly recalls the confessional box, in which confessor and confessant are rigidly separated in a profoundly unequal arrangement. By engaging with the spiritual authority of a priest, asylum seekers can find religious, moral, and psychological comfort; but, even more importantly, they can also attempt to conceptualize their "identity" through storytelling. They do all this not so much for themselves or to be known to other FAC members, but to be acknowledged on a social and institutional level. The discrimination they faced in their home countries, combined with the credibility of what their voices and bodies convey, is essential for ensuring their asylum application dossier is unassailable in the eyes of the competent authorities.[22]

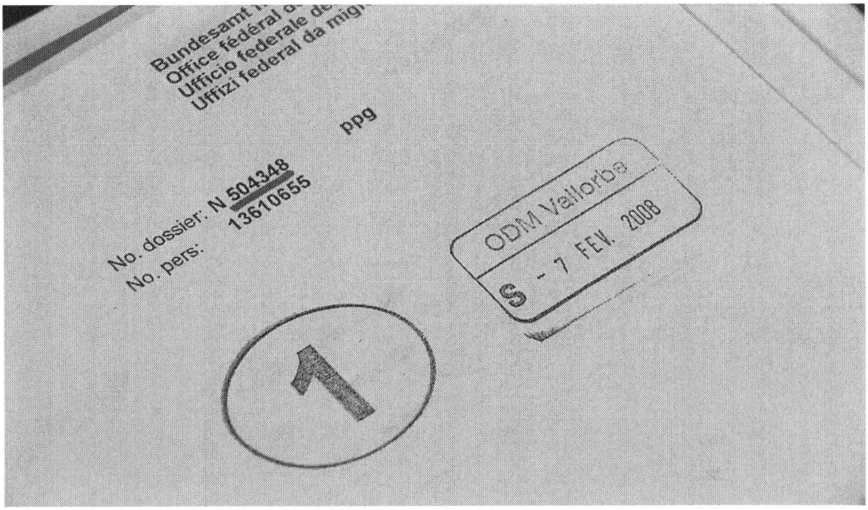

Figure 14. A refugee status application, documenting personal circumstances and grounds for asylum. Still from *The Fortress* (2008).

To confirm this point, in a later sequence the camera shows a detail of a dossier with a photo of the same Somali man: his story has been put down on paper; it has achieved its final form (Figure 14). This time the authority that must accept the migrant's story is no longer the religious and spiritual power of a priest, but that of the officials in charge of assessing the asylum claim. The voices of the two people in charge of evaluating the application point out the "stereotyped" character of this story—composed of gunshots, wounds, and extreme, atrocious acts—and its apparently contradictory aspects. How is it possible to walk for weeks in the desert after having suffered gunshot wounds to the legs?

In the series of encounters with the priest and the public authorities, *The Fortress* highlights the points of overlap between religious and institutional discourse, or at least the risks inherent in their reciprocity. For example, the reading of the Gospels and the conversation with the pastor are oriented toward instructing the man of Somali origin and other migrants on how to use a particular discursive field—a series of words, actions, and figures—that they ultimately adopt and rearticulate more or less explicitly in their narratives. The insistence on the wounds sustained and the display of scars intercepts and reactivates the visual memory of a Christian image rooted in a set of epidermal and bodily figures, from the stigmata to the glorious body of Christ.[23] Moreover, the traces of wounds give possible evidence of the discrimination and violence suffered in one's home country, providing proof of the immediate reason for migration. Yet, as in the case showed by Melgar, when the narrative accentuates its own pathetic register and is colored with nuances that seem excessive or "fictional" to the evaluator, even the power of physical proof can lose legitimacy. What emerges from these sequences of the film is the critical issues involved in the claim and the extreme difficulty of recognizing or not recognizing a political status on the basis of an autobiographical narrative, in which cultural patterns and prejudices weigh on both the teller and the listener.

Against the background of these religiously inspired discursive and figurative models, we perceive the secular character of migration management structures and procedures. However, "secular" should not be confused with the notion of the profane; rather, it represents an area of overlap between the political and religious spheres.[24] Their point of intersection is where we grasp the markedly biopolitical character of border areas: the difference between those who, as citizens, come under the protection of the law and those who enjoy no form of political and legal recognition other than the mere fact of continuing to live—a condition to which charitable, humanitarian aid, and governmental management practices respond.[25] Insofar as the FAC is situated on the margins of the nation, and because it concerns subjects who cannot be framed in terms of citizenship, the facility is a space for articulating pathos—as a demand for, and granting of, intersubjective recognition—and for exercising rhetoric and performing identities, with the aim of fitting into the narrow range of recognition forms available to those who are not Swiss or European citizens. In this sense, the logic of *The Fortress* and Melgar's later films is interesting, because it neither naturalizes nor takes for granted any of the terms or figures by which we tend to name and recognize those who have set out for the European continent, where perhaps part of their family already lives, and, once they reach it, decide to stay and live there.

"Undoing" the refugee seeker means investigating the frames applied to and imposed on migrants. Foucault, the archaeologist of the prison, the asylum, and other total institutions, showed that "mental illness was constituted by all that was said in all the statements that named it, divided it up, described it, explained it, traced its developments, indicated its various correlations, judged it, and possibly gave it speech by articulating, in its name, discourses that were to be taken as its own."[26] Similarly, Melgar investigates and exhibits the system of architectural spaces, rules, practices, social discourses, technologies, and visual cultures that contribute to the construction of a regular or irregular migrant, as an emblematic figure of the contemporary world. As we have seen in previous sections of this chapter, observing internees through the frame of a window is a way to invite the spectator to reflect on the ways an expression—the FAC considered as a "border mediascaping" facility—constitutes its own content: the illegality and precariousness of its hosts. The various dialogues and interviews shown in the film serve as an invitation to consider other mechanisms of institutional framing and sanctioning, such as those determining who is worthy of asylum and who must be forcibly repatriated, and those that package a traumatic experience and turn it into a discourse to make it fit into the regime of asylum rights.[27]

Without necessarily having to wait for the passage of time and the judgment of history, *The Fortress* casts an anachronistic gaze on the present: we see a paradigmatic structure of our time as if we were observing the working mechanism of something that took place in the past. Put even more simply, when we watch the films made by Melgar between 2008 and 2012, intended to analyze how migratory phenomena are managed, it is as though we find ourselves in the halls of the Ellis Island National Museum of Immigration in New York or, even better, on a cinematic itinerary into the Fortress Europe of the new millennium.

Open Circuit

As always when dealing with sensitive issues, critical remarks about Melgar's cinema and his specific positioning in reference to what he documents are always in order. What is the political stance of this filmmaker who never gives himself away in the course of the film, and who apparently seeks to revive an "objective," unbiased idea of the cinematic gaze—"committed but not militant"?[28] However, if that is his intention, then why does he indiscriminately show the lives of people forced to stay inside the FAC as well as those who work in the governmental machine itself?

To borrow one of Bill Nichols's definitions, one could speak of *The Fortress* as an "observational documentary," "with no voice-over commentary, no supplementary music or sound effects, no intertitles, no historical reenactments, no behavior repeated for the camera, and not even any interviews."[29] The observational documentary gives the impression that "What we saw was what there was, or so it seemed."[30] The director tends not to show himself and not to make his voice heard, to the full advantage of the spaces and events that take place in front of the camera. This concept of cinema carries multiple risks and is likely to produce misunderstandings. Observing what happens in front of the camera does not necessarily lead to understanding it, much less to developing a critical response.

Delving deeper, we discover that Melgar's work finds an implicit, yet compelling, point of comparison within the history of cinema—most notably in the oeuvre of Frederick Wiseman, a master of documentary filmmaking, whose work has consistently focused on both observing and understanding the intelligence and shortcomings of public institutions. His filmography includes experiments such as *Titicut Follies* (1967), filmed at Bridgewater Massachusetts State Hospital for the Criminally Insane; *High School* (1968), shot at the Northeast High School in Philadelphia; *Law and Order* (1969) and *Hospital* (1970), following the members of the Kansas City Police Department; and many others, such as *City Hall* (2020), on the government and civic life of Boston. However, if we compare the FAC with these examples, the institution that Melgar documents is different from any school, hospital, or prison located inside national boundaries and intended for the country's citizens. A migration management center is a space of overlapping geographical and historical maps structured on an intercontinental scale—hence the need for an "archaeology of the Fortress." As we have seen, the FAC does not have an organic relationship with the social life of the city or the region in which it is located. Rather, it serves to create a disconnection from the local context, opening to a wider geography that includes other, similar structures and infrastructures designed to repatriate illegal migrants. Melgar breaks down the spaces and management protocols and situations that take shape in the FAC by choosing specific types of shots that isolate certain details to the detriment of others. For example, he develops the narrative entirely in the vicinity of the facility, putting everything around it out of focus. He resorts to the shot/countershot technique and others generally used for fictional films. He does not do this for the sake of fragmentation or experimentation per se, but to analyze and understand the dynamic, stratified environment of an institution that assumes functions of discipline and control over subjects deprived of their citizenship rights and placed in political limbo. Expressed in other terms, the direction and editing are designed to investigate the FAC as a border facility that frames, stages, and sanctions the figure of the asylum seeker. Through this kind of investigative and deconstructive orientation, the film brings into discussion the procedures, discourses, and images of migration.[31]

As has been noted, *The Fortress* shows that "space determines gestures and behaviors, but at the same time it does not totally predict them, it does not definitively contain them. Precisely because of this, the body subject to the political power of spaces and words always presents a remainder, an unassimilable that then reveals its complexity."[32] Accordingly, explicit gestures of resistance emerge in the film's finale: in the migrants' attempts to leave traces of their paths that cannot be capitalized or erased in the bureaucratic procedures for obtaining refugee status, but which assume a posthumous value, like a political certificate of existence or writing left on a wall. Melgar's ability to show both the functional processes of refugee status recognition and the migrants' moments of rest, wasted time, gestures, and individual everyday postures lends his gaze a sense of openness. Although his camera works within institutional space, it is not embedded within the governmental frame of the Vallorbe center. Its testimonial power resides precisely in this gap, with its capacity to critically remediate the regime of the visible and the utterable as it pertains to the FAC, pushing it out of the closed circuit of the institution. Rather than constituting an external critique of the institutional machine, Melgar penetrates its infrastructure and allows the cinematographic device to form a dialectical, intermedial relationship with that of the FAC. Through observation, a reflection matures on forms of contemporary migratory management, thus becoming a political stance.[33]

The documentary character of this cinema piece does not arise from an impression of objectivity as it chronicles the natural unfolding of real and dramatic events. It emerges from the ability to investigate the old and new technologies of power—from windows to surveillance cameras, searches to fingerprints, confessions to trial documentation—through which borders are drawn continuously at different scales. A documentary is not defined by the transparency or invisibility of the cinematographic eye, but by its ability to show the spectator the work of the discursive and visual frames in the construction of subjects and objects, and therefore the mechanisms through which the reality of the migratory phenomena of the new millennium is imagined and managed. The structure of a fortress is made as much of technologies, images, and words as it is of bricks.

CHAPTER 4

EMBODIED BORDERS AND CUSTOMIZED BODIES

À Calais

"No, not you! This afternoon it was Laurent Cantet, last week Michael Haneke, and Charlie Winston's been here as well. So, no, Monsieur Carrère, not you! That's what we say here: we've had enough of these 'People'—excuse the word—who come to Calais to earn their bread and who treat those of us trapped inside like laboratory rats! What have you come here for?"[1] This quotation comes from the opening pages of a reportage in Calais by the French writer, screenwriter, and film director Emmanuel Carrère, written for the January 2016 issue of *Revue XXI*. It comes across almost as an *excusatio non petita,* a rhetorical strategy adopted by a prominent author of contemporary literature as he takes a moment for self-reflexive inquiry before launching into a cogent but overused issue of our day. How, indeed, does one set off once again to Lampedusa, Lesvos, or Calais—where Europe's management of the migratory phenomenon opens enormous individual and social wounds—without participating in the political and moral economy of catastrophe, perennially revived and rebroadcast in images?

This chapter focuses on the films shot by French filmmaker Sylvain George from the early 2000s in the municipality of Calais, on the English Channel, in the continental strip closest to Great Britain.[2] A town historically marked by its strategic location, Calais has been a tempting target for occupation or governance. Since the fourteenth century, it has been besieged multiple times, taken over by the British as an outpost, occupied by Spain, recaptured by France, invaded by Nazi Germany, and liberated by the

Canadian army. As the gateway to the Eurotunnel since 1994, with the migratory phenomena of the new millennium it first became the site of the Sangatte identification center and then an area of multiple makeshift encampments known popularly as "The Jungle."[3] The area was dismantled by the police in 2016, without providing adequate shelter for the people who lived there.

George's on-site work has extended over weeks, months, and years. His work is based on planned and unplanned meetings aimed at collecting direct testimonies from migrants and connecting lost memories, lost objects, and details that escape the naked eye. Over the next few pages, it will become clear that George is equally interested in showing the intrusiveness of border control technologies and exploring forms of resistance by migrants. His cinema extends and adds complexity to the idea of the border mediascape by considering practices of communication, interaction, and camouflage developed by people forced to live in border areas.

Following this interpretive path, the next section focuses on the theoretical and practical issue of the "apparatus" *(dispositif)*: a recurrent topic in George's cinema and a key notion for political philosophy, which characterizes power technologies as something from which it is almost impossible to escape. From this it becomes clear that control devices tend to exert a totalizing hold on the border mediascape; however, attempts made by migrants to escape their grasp and unexpected "alliances" also emerge, thus producing a dynamic model of these geopolitical areas. The third and fourth sections focus on palm printing and fingerprinting as a biopolitical technology designed to impose a certain geopolitical regime. This issue is explicitly shown or implicitly present in several films devoted to contemporary migration. I limit myself to mentioning *Just About My Fingers* (2012) and *Land of Transit* (*Terra di transito,* 2014) by Paolo Martino, and *I Am Dublin* (*Jag är Dublin,* 2015) by Ahmed Abdullahi, David Aronowitsch, Sharmarke Binyusuf, and Anna Persson. An analysis of the most extraordinary sequences in George's cinema guides us to reflect on the surface of the migrants' bodies as a battleground between the violence of governmental strategies and the extreme character of resistance tactics. With these insights, through the same sequences, the multiple character of migrant gestures of resistance emerges, revealing an anachronistic temporality and an anatopistic spatiality—the ability to critically connect the present time, in the European context, with the colonial past.

The chapter concludes with a coda on Auguste Rodin's statue *The Burghers of Calais,* to which George dedicates a long sequence in *Fragments,* thereby establishing an association between the city's urban landscape, its monuments, and the condition of those who, illegally, are forced to camp on its margins. In this sequence George establishes a relation between the techniques of molding and casting as features of sculptural and visual art and contemporary biometric apparatuses.

Through the Apparatus

George's practice as a filmmaker is intentionally theoretical and militant. As can also be inferred from his output as a writer, the French director's work refers explicitly to the thought of Walter Benjamin, Hannah Arendt, and other political philosophers.[4] The title *May They Rest in Revolt* is taken from Henri Michaux's 1949 poem "Qu'ils reposent en révolte."[5] Right from the start, the film offers an audiovisual critical reflection on the notion of the apparatus. This philosophical concept, originating in the second half of the twentieth century, describes the various forms and techniques employed over time to discipline and control living beings. As is well-known, the question of the apparatus has been central to Michel Foucault's thought since the 1970s. Foucault aimed to define

> firstly, a thoroughly heterogeneous ensemble consisting of discourses, institutions, architectural forms, regulatory decisions, laws, administrative measures, scientific statements, philosophical, moral and philanthropic propositions—in short, the said as much as the unsaid. . . . Secondly, what I am trying to identify in this apparatus is precisely the nature of the connection that can exist between these heterogeneous elements. . . . Thirdly, I understand by the term "apparatus" *[dispositif]* a sort of—shall we say—formation which has as its major function at a given historical moment that of responding to an urgent need.[6]

George's camera shows the conditions of those whose lives are hunted by apparatuses. As discussed in previous chapters, migrants are subjected to multiple institutional practices and discourses that affect their lives and determine their status. Being a migrant in Calais seems to require that one develop a paranoid attitude, characterized by a generalized suspicion of any spatial context. This includes the fear that any architectural structure could incorporate a form of remote control and the apprehension that any infrastructure adjacent to the Eurotunnel may belong to the border management system. As Giorgio Agamben notes in his summary of the "question of the apparatus," the development and widespread application of technological and biometric devices marks the transition to a state of permanent control. This era of constant surveillance extinguishes the dialectic between closure and openness, constraint and freedom, favoring the former: "By developing and perfecting anthropometric technologies invented in the nineteenth century in order to identify recidivist criminals (from mug shots to fingerprinting), surveillance by means of video cameras transforms the public space of the city into the interior of an immense prison."[7]

Over the last few decades, contemporary philosophy and media studies have continuously sought ways out of the impasse of the apparatus, a way to escape its pervasive and totalizing character. Through the idea of "profanation," described as "the counter-apparatus that restores to common use what sacrifice had separated and divided,"[8] Agamben has developed something akin to a theoretical sleight of hand. If "to profane" means to return something that has been placed in a separate sphere to common use, then profanation, when speaking of apparatuses, can be understood as reappropriating what has been captured and made inaccessible to us. Although Agamben does not provide examples, it seems fruitful to draw inspiration from his concept to describe and analyze George's films and the ways migrants knock out or circumvent the apparatus in their effort to escape its totalizing grip or, at the very least, to pass through it.

The real problem with the notion of apparatus, making it difficult to evade, is that any practice, object, or technology can operate as one. Even George's camera qualifies as an apparatus, just like the media system that will circulate the images of migrants captured in border areas. In the opening of Carrère's reportage, writers, photojournalists, and filmmakers arrive in Calais with their cameras, computers, pens, notebooks, and other means for producing media content. They do so to witness, denounce, and challenge how people who choose to change their lives and cross borders, often with no other viable alternatives, face the multiplication and proliferation of even more borders. These artists venture to the frontier because they realize that a drama of enormous magnitude is unfolding. They want to share and transmit this experience to others, fostering something like a collective consciousness "about the migrant drama." But how can they accomplish this without reverting to a discourse that clearly separates *subject* from *object* or, more precisely, audiovisual apparatuses from living beings, now viewed as "bare life"?[9] How does one avert the risk that simply witnessing these events will eventually serve as a control mechanism? And then, even when this witnessing does seem to open up a space for "migrants," how can one ensure that this act does not actually reintegrate their personal and political experiences into the creation of a specific discourse and visual framework, thereby limiting their movement and assigning them a predefined position in it?

More than other contemporary artists, filmmakers, and photographers, George is acutely aware of these issues. In his writings, he has reflected explicitly on the difficult relationship between those who arrive on the scene to document events and those directly involved, who are often left without a voice.[10] To avoid falling into the apparatus trap, George has focused on transforming the cinematographic frame and all forms of audiovisual language into a tactical space aimed at neutralizing governmental strategies, image by image. As I will explain in the following pages, *May They Rest in Revolt* makes visible the practices migrants employ to turn border apparatuses against themselves. This is only possible because the film itself is conceived of as an affirmative instrument for the "profanation" of the technological regime of border control.

At a primary thematic level, the movie camera addresses the migratory phenomenon by reconceptualizing it as both highly

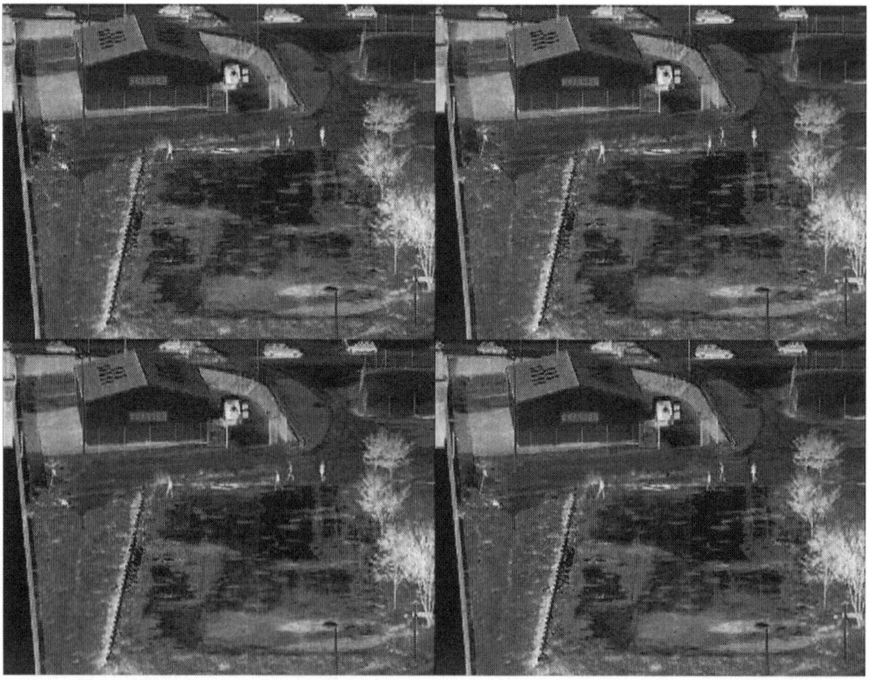

Figure 15. Forms of control over urban spaces in the city of Calais. Still from *May They Rest in Revolt* (2010).

ethical and political.[11] It documents the hiding places of migrants and their tragic attempts to pass through the coastal fences near embarkation points or to sneak into the double bottom of trucks continually crossing the Channel. Although migrants are prohibited from accessing the entrance to the Channel Tunnel, these routes remain open to vehicles transporting goods between France and the United Kingdom. As a result, some migrants attempt to join the transport convoys—at great personal risk—in order to cross the border undetected. This context has already been investigated in other cinematographic, photographic, and artistic projects carried out in the area—above all, in *Calais: The Last Border* (2003) by Marc Isaacs, *Border* (2004) by Laura Waddington, and *Kalès* (2017) by Laurent Van Lancker. In the same geographical area, visual artist Matthieu Pernot brought his own photographic equipment, challenging the limits of the notion of apparatus and seeking to effectively document the migrants' lives.[12] George shows us the flow of everyday life between Calais and The Jungle: we see discussions, meals cooked and shared, stops at a public fountain, restorative baths in the city canal, and so forth. Out of this an everyday geography takes shape, consisting of recurrent, ever-changing places. Thanks to these kinds of images, we can recognize the social and political bonds that survive in refugee camps. These exceptional spaces serve as experimental laboratories for alternative forms of sociality and politics.[13]

On a secondary level, the exclusive use of high-contrast, black-and-white frames in *May They Rest in Revolt* and other films elevates George's inquiry into a diagnosis of the border's sensorial regime. The exaggerated formalism of his composition simulates border control apparatuses and related methods of visualizing space and motion, such as surveillance cameras, infrared cameras, thermal sensors, and so on. A series of visual effects—ranging from black and white to reversal between positive and negative image, from slow motion to split screen—accentuate the graphic nature of the media representation. The film reveals that various technologies, differing in sophistication and visibility to the naked eye, function to monitor spaces and define differentiated conditions of access (Figure 15). In this respect, George's research anticipates, or at least resonates with, the work of artist Richard Mosse and his multi-channel installation *Incoming* (2014–17). This piece maps the movement of migrants across the Middle East, North Africa, and Europe using technology originally designed for surveillance, which records thermal motion.[14] Although the complexity of such a project warrants its own study, I will limit myself to the main critical interpretation: Mosse reveals what it means to "see like a State." By that, he means "to enter a thermal imaginary in which the 'human' figures as a subject that is either to be destroyed as a target (the camera is in fact classified as a weapons system), or to be in need of rescue, either from peril on the sea or (in the dominant, state-sanctioned narrative) from those who place them in peril on the sea, the 'traffickers.'"[15]

On a third level, by filming in black and white and using over- and underexposure, George affirmatively reconceptualizes the border mediascape. He presents it as something migrants continually relate to, experience, and are a part of. Instead of simulating control technologies, the tendency toward abstract composition of the film frame restores the experimental, affirmative potential of interactions among the inhabitants of these geographical areas. This is how the camera engages with the Calais environment, alternately moving away and coming closer to all the things piled up around the refugee camp: the garbage, the vegetation, the waves of the sea, the foam left behind by the waves, and so forth (Figure 16).[16]

This dual meaning of black and white, along with the film's composition, is also evident in George's other films, such as *Paris Is a Movable Feast: A Film in 18 Waves* (*Paris est une fête: Un film en 18 vagues,* 2017). In this film, the twinkling lights of the city and the green spaces of the *sans papiers* camp offer an occasion for unexpected visionary sequences. This approach is also found in *Obscure Night: Wild Leaves* (*Nuit obscure: Feuillets sauvages,* 2022), *Obscure Night: Goodbye Here, Anywhere* (*Nuit obscure: Au revoir ici, n'importe où,* 2023), and *Obscure Night: Ain't I a Child?* (*Nuit obscure: Ain't I a Child?,* 2025). In these films, too, George continually intertwines documentation and experimentation, lending several shots a distinctly graphic character. Both the 2022 and the 2023 films explore the border areas of Melilla, investigated in *Those Who Jump* by Abou Bakar Sidibé, Moritz Siebert, and Estephan Wagner, discussed in the introduction, and in several other films, such as *Tell Me When . . .* (2011) by Steffen Köhn and Paola Calvo, *The Land Between* (2014) by David Fedele, *Riski* (2017) by Otto Reuschel, and *Harraga: Those Who Burn Their Lives* (2023) by Benjamin Rost. These films reveal the living conditions of those known in Moroccan and Algerian Arabic as the *harraga*: the migrants who burn their documents to prevent identification by European authorities. More broadly, it signifies the radical experience of crossing the border, marking an indelible life passage.

To sum up, George's cinema investigates possible connections between migrants' resistance and the environmental dynamics that characterize the European continental edge: the wind, the waves of the sea crashing ashore, seaweed, bushes, and so many other forms of interaction and transformation between differ-

Figure 16. A collection of objects on sand reflects the dynamic character of the Calais border environment, shaped by continuous interaction between various elements. Still from *May They Rest in Revolt* (2010).

ent elements and organisms. As highlighted by Debarati Sanyal, George's camera "weaves multiple elements of Calais's borderscape into a ever-shifting tapestry in which living organisms, atmospheric phenomena, the elements, and inanimate things are in constant, nonhierarchical interaction."[17] These landscape references are mostly to the English Channel, but as noted in other studies, we also find shots of "barren mountains, misty passes, natural walls, and spaces of intense light reduced to signs of alteration and instability fix points of origin with respect to distant lands and migrants' home territories."[18] As *May They Rest in Revolt* progresses, the acts of fleeing from the police and camouflaging to escape control apparatuses resonate with the Channel environment, portrayed as something elusive and difficult to manage in its totality. If the apparatuses are justified by their mandate to blend with the geographical boundary and control every movement on this continental threshold, the film portrays this claim as profoundly reactionary. This attitude inevitably lags behind the creativity of the ecological assemblages typical of an area with strong environmental dynamism. From this film, we receive an image of Calais as a front line, as a space of conflict and relationship, where all the natural elements and various entities participate.

The gestures of the people encamped in Calais are part of a complex environmental system in which the personal and social lives of migrants, banished and forced into illegality, develop through continuous experimentation with forms of living and dwelling. This aspect, present in all George's films—the idea that migrants form a kind of aesthetic vanguard, understood as both a sensory and political experience—is as interesting as it is potentially problematic, as it subjects bodies and the environment as a whole to a continuous aestheticization.[19] Migrants are able to reconnect spheres typically seen as separate: the "natural" environment versus public and social life. In the words of Jacques Rancière, one of the first critics to recognize the profundity of George's cinema, it "does not merely bear witness to the struggle of these migrants. It also offers them the sensitive world that corresponds to them."[20] It is a world, the philosopher continues, "where there are not only makeshift tents, cold, hunger, and barriers but also their transmutation into ever-changing spectacles, into movements and mirrorings, into shadows and reflections. This is the deepest political sense of Sylvain George's films."[21]

In short, the images in *May They Rest in Revolt* do not merely express the director's point of view or that of the individual protagonists, yet they also do not align with a panoptic faculty of control—"the Apparatus"—that can transform the world entirely into an object. Making films amid extreme precarity and political violence does not mean positioning oneself "outside" the influence of contemporary political technologies or "inside" one's own pure artistic consciousness. The goal is to expose the invisibility of the border, understand how it works, and identify the unexpected intersectional alliances that form within the border mediascape.[22] George's exploration passes through the apparatus and goes beyond the impasse created by this notion, as the film frame is seen as a surface for reciprocally mediating and defining different entities. In other words, the film allows an alternative conception of the Calais environment to emerge, showing it not as unilaterally fabricated by the apparatus but as the result of a continuous process of "individuation," an activity of perpetual becoming.[23]

Film mediation lies in between: it explores and uncovers the mutual interdependence and differentiation of what we commonly call subjects and objects, along with many other possible forms of subordination, all within a shared horizon. George's camera surfaces through bodies, tree leaves, sea sand, and the foam of the waves. This gaze matures in the "sensitive world" Rancière describes, a spectacle of transformation and difference made of shadows, mirrorings, and reflections. It disproportionately extends the notion of the border mediascape, oscillating between "national frontier," "continental fault line," and "ecosystem."

Biometrics and the Paradox of an Affirmative Necropolitics

At the heart of *May They Rest in Revolt* are two sequences that remain particularly impressed in the viewer's memory. These vivid, shocking sequences lucidly describe the invasiveness of contemporary governmental practices and illustrate the techno-aesthetic nature of biopolitical apparatuses.

Framed in detail, sharply contrasted in black and white, are a man's hands. He is carrying a disposable razor blade. He brings it close to the fingers of his left hand and slowly begins to wound the fingertips. Rather than clean cuts, he makes a twisting motion that shows some skill, even in the extreme gesture of self-mutilation. A film montage intervenes to detail the man's fingers: not a drop of blood emerges, but rather a series of marks that furrow the flesh and lift the epidermis. Then, framed in the medium shot, from bottom to top, is Temesghen, an Eritrean migrant repeatedly referenced by George in his films and texts, who intervenes with a provocative metaphor to denounce the immunitary character of European borders: "We have to survive in Europe.

This is a virus. HIV virus, this is virus in Europe."[24] Immediately below, another man, again framed from the bottom up, explains the meaning of this defacement: "Europeans have developed a system to centralize fingerprints in order to know how and where you arrive and where you go. If the Europeans have developed their techniques, we have developed our techniques to hide our fingerprints." He refers to the Dublin Convention, active since September 1997, and subsequent regulations, establishing that asylum-seeker fingerprints have to be taken and stored in the Eurodac system. The EU state where the fingerprints are taken is responsible for the refugee's asylum claim.[25] This is a technical way of saying that, once migrants are fingerprinted, it becomes impossible for them to continue their journey, join their family, or pursue their plans in another European country. Temesghen again intervenes, stating that "if it was possible to cut this one [the right hand], throw it and bring another one I will be doing that." And then he continues, arguing that "they make us slaves, the slaves of their country through these fingerprints. They destroy our lives, we cannot go, we cannot change our lives." A slow fade to black closes the first sequence and opens the next.

Now, from a close position, one observes a fire in a brazier. A series of indistinct voices hint at the presence of a group of men all around it. A long metal screw is held in contact with the flame on the end of a looped wire. Then, shown in detail, someone places the glowing screw on a wooden board and begins to touch it. He touches it with his index finger, ring finger and middle finger, his little finger and thumb. The screw returns to the fire as a second man and then a third, whose faces we never see, repeat the same operation. The camera lingers on the details and allow us to glimpse the white streaks on the open palms caused by the screw threadings (Figure 17). Suddenly, amid the noises accompanying the passing of the wire from hand to hand, a voice is heard: "I say this is our tradition." All around, laughter erupts among the group members. "Because white men used to . . . they did it with our great-grandparents." After a brief pause he continues: "Now we are not going to wait somebody to pain ourselves. I will pain ourselves." As the camera shows details of a series of completely striped hands by the glowing screw, the voices turn to

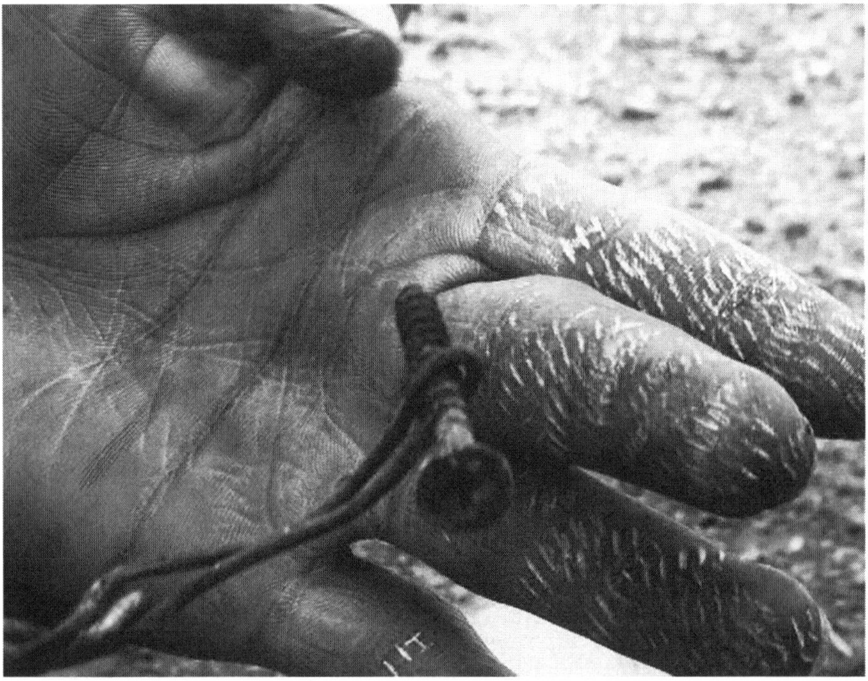

Figure 17. Migrants remove their fingerprints and create new traces on the palms of their hands. Still from *May They Rest in Revolt* (2010).

the underlying causes of such practices, and thus to the mechanisms governing the collection of fingerprints and other personal data. Then, amid many other sentences, as the screw continues to be pulled over fingers, one of the two voices says: "It is very painful, but what can we do? What can we do? What can we do?" Then, the other voice envision a reversal of power relations: "This will stop one day. One day Africa will become like Europe and Europe like Africa! One day Europeans will migrate to Africa in search of work." After that, voices begin repeating "Africa united" and "Africa proudest!" as if to relaunch the moment of collective elation.[26]

These sequences, however stark, cannot be interpreted in their collective dimension as a manifestation of nihilism. Rather, they show that the migrants are fully aware of how the technologies governing borders work: by intervening on bodies.[27] They depict the painful maturation of a choice of resistance, understood as an extreme act of self-harm aimed at neutralizing the prehensile nature of biometric apparatuses.[28] The apparatus in question is the identification through palm prints and fingerprints, a *dispositif* as contemporary as it is modern, developed from the late-nineteenth-century studies of Francis Galton, a naturalist and eugenics advocate. This apparatus is deeply anchored in a positivist epistemology, by which a trace is tantamount to the identification of an origin, a precise identity, and therefore an attribution of responsibility.[29] What becomes evident here is the imbalance structuring contemporary borders, giving rise to all forms of discrimination and racialization. We also witness the act of profaning or tactically defacing the legal apparatus of the Dublin Convention and the technological apparatus of Eurodac. The film shows the inherent "coldness" of palm-print devices used for registering people. These devices purport to match a life and delineate its boundaries of action and movement through the wavy lines on a hand. The coldness is then warmed by a live fire and a blade. This kind of temperature disturbance in the border mediascape appears to be just as eagerly pursued by the migrants as it is painful for them.[30]

This practice of fingerprint removal can be likened to what Banu Bargu has called the "weaponization of life," with reference to hunger strikes, sewing of lips and eyelids, and other forms of self-harm under conditions of detention or restriction of their rights. In these tactics "the body is utilized as the conduit of a political intervention," even though, as she points out, an intervention of this kind is "irreducible to the corporeality of the body."[31] The idea of transforming life into a weapon may be misunderstood. Also, it may not be clear how it applies to the situation described earlier. Such weaponization does not occur by turning the body into a threat to others. Instead, the threat targets parts of one's body where apparatuses focus and enforce their logic. The weaponization extends beyond the body, threatening the fingerprinting device and, consequently, the corresponding biopolitical, social, and legal systems.

In her book, Bargu describes similar practices as forms of "necroresistance." These are practices that both resist the violence exerted through apparatuses and are self-harming in themselves.[32] The *May They Rest in Revolt* sequence suggests it is possible to adopt this concept and develop it further in the paradoxical terms of an "affirmative necropolitics." We first encountered the hypothesis of an affirmative reconception of technologies used for biopolitical control in chapter 1, in the context of sea rescues and medical care on the island of Lampedusa, where the border was reconceived as a dynamic space in which "life would no longer be the object but somehow the subject of politics."[33] In contrast, this sequence presents something more akin to a paradoxical affirmative reconception of the necropolitical proposed by Achille Mbembe, as discussed in earlier chapters.[34] The necropolitical concept aims to underline the deep-rooted and enduring relationship between sovereignty and the right to life or death in the contemporary biopolitical landscape. This idea is made tangible by the choices of democratic states to allow thousands of migrants to die at the borders of their territorial waters, along mountain ridges, or on other geographic and political frontiers, all under the operational gaze of control technologies. This notion goes far beyond explicit acts of execution, serving to identify the various forms of violence systematically tolerated or exercised by national and supranational authorities.

"Affirmative necropolitics" is paradoxical because it reappropriates a concept linked to violence and death, transforming it into an act that affirms individual or collective agency and power. The issue here is similar to the right to self-inflicted violence to prevent large-scale political violence. Clearly, we cannot lose sight of the extreme nature of such resistance, which the migrants themselves express when they talk about their pain, suffering, and lack of alternatives. Equally crucial are the critical issues in interpreting these gestures: the risk of normalizing violence and death in political discourse and the danger of romanticizing acts born of desperation. At the same time, these resistance practices do not derive their meaning from self-mutilation itself, nor from the public and media exposure of suffering bodies. Instead, their strength lies in the determination to bring physical harm closer to themselves. This effort seeks to disable the apparatuses through which life is regulated and death is distributed occasionally but systematically along Europe's borders.

Biometric technologies aim to link traces on hands with a fixed and unequivocal idea of origin, identity, and destiny. In contrast, these bodily gestures and techniques assert a rejection: the right of individuals not to coincide with their own imprint or control image. This challenges the technological, scientific, and legal systems called on to limit and repress political life through biological data. The affirmative character of such practices lies in rejecting and overthrowing the apparatuses that daily suspend fundamental rights. It is a counterattack on what I called the "media color line" in the introduction.

Techno-aesthetics and politics are more intertwined than ever in this instance. This tactic develops and matures specifically by identifying the operational mode of fingerprinting technology. It focuses on the body in order to push beyond it, challenging what seeks to map, identify, match it with a stable image. Bargu explains in her book that "the weaponization of life, understood as a form of expression, also invites us to complicate our understanding of violence by restoring an independent role to form as having distinctive qualities, certain political and ethical effects of its own."[35] Emphasizing these practices' expressive forms or their techno-aesthetic component in no way diminishes their political character. In fact, only when we arrive at a specific understanding of this character of contemporary borders can we understand how they operate and how to evade them, uncovering potential forms of profanation of the frontier.

If the biological characteristics of the human body are instrumentalized for identification and discrimination, it becomes crucial to recognize and value the body's inherent openness, its readiness to reshape itself and hybridize with the external environment. Temesghen's words from the first part of the sequence come to mind. He mentions the possibility of replacing one's own hand with another to bypass the identification and constraints imposed by the device based on biological data. It involves envisaging the body as a process rather than a given, and the flesh, its biological substrate, as a sensible threshold of articulation.

Affirmative necropolitics both illustrates the challenge of finding ways to escape and shows the willingness of people ensnared in its grip to take any action to undermine the apparatus and create the conditions for a trans-individual affirmation.

Here and Elsewhere

Watching the campfire sequence over and over, I get the impression that the migrants feel the need to liberate themselves from more than just the fingerprinting devices. Suddenly, in the midst of the sequence described earlier, the protagonists feel observed. They sense the presence of someone who, despite having won their trust, remains an outsider: Sylvain George's gaze. This impression is bolstered by the diary where George describes making this part of the film: "It's the African camp, Eritreans, a few Ghanaians, Cameroonians. . . . I approach them. Around the campfires, they are all gathered. Heads turn towards me. Anxious glances. Many don't know me. Others recognize me immediately. I can stay here. With them. Without the camera. Around the fires."[36] I believe his decision to only film the details of this episode, without revealing individual identities, took shape as he came to understand the extreme and particularly significant nature of the moment. He grasped the opportunity to observe and document outside the subject-object opposition, choosing not to position himself as the director who frames the scene by bringing his eye close to the viewfinder. Instead, he experiments with an immanent cinema, made as if it were "without a camera." I also have the impression that one of the migrants senses that customizing their palms and fingers could evoke, in the eyes of external viewers, a stereotypical imaginary of Africa, made up of ritual practices and collective body modifications around a fire. It is a risky imagery, since it could degrade, delegitimize, or even racialize their gesture of resistance. Thus, as this awareness surfaces, instead of allowing all this to flow into the camera screen and be instrumentalized in the cinema and media information system, the migrants reappropriate and reorient it. As we have seen in the description of the sequence, one of them explicitly mentions their great-grandparents and the idea of "tradition." After a burst of laughter from the others, he redirects the conversation to the issue of colonialism, and to the specific forms of control and violence inflicted on the bodies.

In the political and social sciences, special attention has been paid to migrants' acts of resistance to border management technologies. When discussing practices like the one shown in the film, researchers have noted the importance of understanding and underscoring their political significance in the context of contemporary border management. As has been pointed out, migrants' gestures of struggle must first resist "being homogenized and categorized into the broader groups that oppressors attempt to fit them into (e.g., along racial/ethnic lines), by practicing and sharing their cultural diversity."[37] However, while scientific and critical discourse has sometimes encountered difficulties dealing with the layered intensity of such gestures, the cinematographic gaze has the ability to do these gestures justice, by restoring their complexity.

In my view, the temporality and spatiality of the sequence filmed by George is particularly multifaceted, which allows the migrants to dissect, express, and reframe it in a political context. To start, we have the overt content of the sequence: the practice of fingerprint removal as a form of resistance to the biometric devices of the new millennium, as described in the previous section. Next, we have the analogical meaning: the fact that this practice takes on the appearance of scarification, where traces are created by cutting the skin with sharp tools and introducing substances into the wound to alter its shape and prevent infection. This risks evoking images of traditional rituals in viewers, with potential cultural or racial connotations. Finally, as evident from the offscreen voice of the migrant who first says "This is our tradition" and then shifts the subject with "Because white men used to . . . they did it with our grandparents and great-grandparents," this practice demonstrates the persistence of colonial-era violence on bodies. Indeed, as has been noted, "the evocation of slavery in this scene is not symbolic, but utterly material, for the contemporary politics of migration and its biometric controls 'literally' brands migrants, marking their bodies within a European economy of recognition and forcing them to brand themselves in response."[38]

The "tradition" mentioned in the first sentence should not be understood as referring to a static identity. It alludes, rather, to what Walter Benjamin termed the "tradition of the oppressed," understood as the memory of violence suffered by a multitude of individuals and populations across various places and times.[39] Just as in recent centuries the bodies and skin of the colonized were subjected to the violence of the color line apparatus, today fingerprints are taken. Just as forms of resistance and the overthrow of power relations were experienced then, today the struggle continues.[40] This route clarifies the idea of an "Africa united," as mentioned by the migrants in the final sequence, and makes the transformation of a tradition of the oppressed into a form of political awareness and struggle extremely clear. As Frantz Fanon reminds us, "Africa united" was a "vague formula, yet one to which the men and women of Africa were passionately attached, and whose operative value served to bring immense pressure to bear on colonialism."[41] This same formula becomes the motto for those who, while evoking a colonial memory, at the same time challenge the notion in the new millennium that the lines on one's fingers represent a form of destiny, a border inscribed on the body.

Customizing palms does more than merely impair the identificatory capabilities of border apparatuses; it also serves as a form of expression and recognition. Without ever showing the faces and identities of individual migrants, George's camera accomplishes two things: it reveals the practice through which migrants erase a geography that imposes itself on territories and bodies, and it shows their act of writing an alternative geography. The film depicts a multilayered practice whose political power derives precisely from its layers, enabling the connections between "now" and "then" and "here" and "elsewhere" to be recognized.

Compared to the ability of border media apparatuses to impose their notions of time and space through history and geography, gestures of resistance manifest as images that are *anachronistic,* out of chronological time, or *anatopistic,* outside a regimented concept of space.[42] These "displaced" images compel us to critically examine the geopolitical hierarchies of borders established during colonialism and still prevailing around the world today.[43]

The palms of the migrants shown in *May They Rest in Revolt* conjure images of distant memories and places while simultaneously asserting their dramatic presence in contemporary Europe. Those who decide to redraw the lines on their hands make no claim to identity or iconoclasm with their gesture, then. No attempt to establish an identity through biometric technologies can ever define a life.

Coda: *The Burghers of Calais*

I conclude this chapter by discussing George's second film shot in Calais, which maintains a certain proximity to *May They Rest in Revolt* by returning to the same places, focusing on the same apparatuses, and allowing the same tactics of resistance and forms of alliance to emerge on camera.

About twenty minutes into *Fragments,* the issue of fingerprints and methods for removing them comes up again. Through montage, George's film creates an apparently incongruous juxtaposition between the gestures and statements of migrants hiding from modern biometric devices and a nineteenth-century work of art located in the center of Calais. We now see a series of shots of the statue created by the renowned French sculptor Auguste Rodin, positioned in front of the town hall (Figure 18). The city commissioned the statue in 1884 to commemorate a historic event from the Hundred Years' War. Six "burghers" (Eustache de Saint Pierre, Jacques and Pierre de Wissant, Jean de Fiennes, Andrieu d'Andres, and Jean d'Aire) appeared before King Edward III of England with nooses around their necks, offering him the keys to the city to persuade him to lift his siege.

It may come as a surprise that, to my knowledge, no critical analysis of Sylvain George's cinema, particularly his study of Calais, has examined the connection between Rodin's sculpture and the apparatuses of border management. It is as if the film's "artistic" sequence, dedicated to a monument, is meant to be kept separate from its political analysis.[44]

The first temptation when confronted with this sequence is to approach it thematically and schematically. One might assume a

Figure 18. Auguste Rodin's *Burghers of Calais,* framed and reinterpreted as a reflection on the possible meanings and functions of the imprint. Still from *Fragments* (2011).

juxtaposition between the history of the burghers of Calais and that of contemporary migrants: their shared precariousness and deprivation, the suspension of their respective rights, and their willingness to sacrifice or assert the political value of giving up their lives. A second temptation is to view this *Fragments* sequence as one among many that George dedicates to public monuments in contemporary European cities.[45] He depicts them as problematic objects, poised between constituted power—which commissioned their construction and legitimizes itself through them—and constituent power, which embodies the memory of past revolutions.

As art history and theory teach us, crucially informing border studies and political theory, understanding Rodin requires an awareness of the paradox inherent in any trace, especially the "imprint." Rodin's works, generally referred to as sculpture, only partly conform to Michelangelo's method of sculpting marble by removing stone from the block. Rodin preferred to mold wax models, create casts, and then assemble figures from several parts, ultimately casting one or more pieces in bronze. Rodin epitomized the romantic ideal of the "last sculptor." At the same time, he experimented with the boundaries of various techniques, such as manipulation, plaster casting, and metal fusion, which had been established over the centuries. His approach to creative work aimed to transcend the notions of "individuality" and "origin," moving toward an idea of artistic practice and the sculptural body characterized by openness and becomingness.

In one of the essays collected in *Other Criteria,* Leo Steinberg points out that Rodin's continual shaping of figures was the necessary condition for inaugurating a process of sculptural composition intended as a process of assemblage and reassemblage: "No Rodin sculpture is known until it is known in its adaptability. Most of his works are constellations of interchangeable parts; and within his enormous output you can play endlessly spotting the vagrants."[46] While observing *The Burghers of Calais,* it seems that the monumental and epic nature of the six figures arises precisely from the exaggerated portrayal of their physical features and gestures. The six bodies are both separate and interconnected; at times, from certain perspectives their individual outlines become indistinguishable to the viewer. The burghers' robes and the ropes and keys held by Jean d'Aire are recognizable as objects yet seamlessly integrated with the bodies. This perspective views historical discourse as a monumentalization of everyday gestures and objects.

In his book on the imprint, Georges Didi-Huberman revisits Steinberg's reflection, noting that

> Rodin's casting is no longer the *thing-substitute* of an absent referent; it is from the outset a *substituting movement,* a figural work of substitution that does not cease, paradigmatically, to generate itself, that is to say, to proliferate by associating, always creating new organic hypotheses that are unthinkable from the point of view of the secular "human figure," which this *work of form* irremediably decomposes.[47]

This observation on Rodin is laden with technological, social, and political implications. It highlights how Europe's greatest sculptor of the nineteenth century deconstructed the positivist notion of the trace. As Galton was laying the groundwork for fingerprints and their use in the judiciary system, Rodin explored the impossible coincidence between the imprint and the objects it purportedly references unambiguously. In doing so, he probed the persistence of a gap, or as Derrida would call it, *différance*.[48]

With Rodin's work in mind, we can weave together some of the threads in George's cinema and reexamine a few theoretical questions. These include the relationship between the cinematic gaze and gestures of resistance, the interplay between biometric technologies and bodies, the connection between apparatuses and forms of life, all from a long-term perspective. We must incorporate art history into our reflections on contemporary technologies of power. As the film camera captures various details of *The Burghers of Calais,* focusing particularly on the expressive hands and rain-soaked palms, the viewer recalls the sequence of the migrants customizing their fingerprints. George's approach of focusing on details, without showing individual faces, creates a trans-individual identity. Opposing the positivist and neopositivist notions of trace and imprint, resisting any imposed ideas of origin or identity, the cinematographic print gains its effectiveness through movement, as it embodies a process of becoming. It unveils the invisibility of borders while simultaneously creating juxtapositions and alliances between entities that are distinct and distant across space and time.

Like Rodin, who was fascinated by the mystery of the hand, modeling and treasuring hundreds of models, George also finds great significance in hands. The most experimental sequences in *May They Rest in Revolt, Fragments,* and *Paris Is a Movable Feast,* blending aesthetic exploration with political demands, always involve the hand. This is perhaps the common fate of artists active during historical moments marked by profound technological change, especially involving "traces" and their political applications. Rodin and George were both challenged to question the power and fragility of the hand, a body part that, more than any

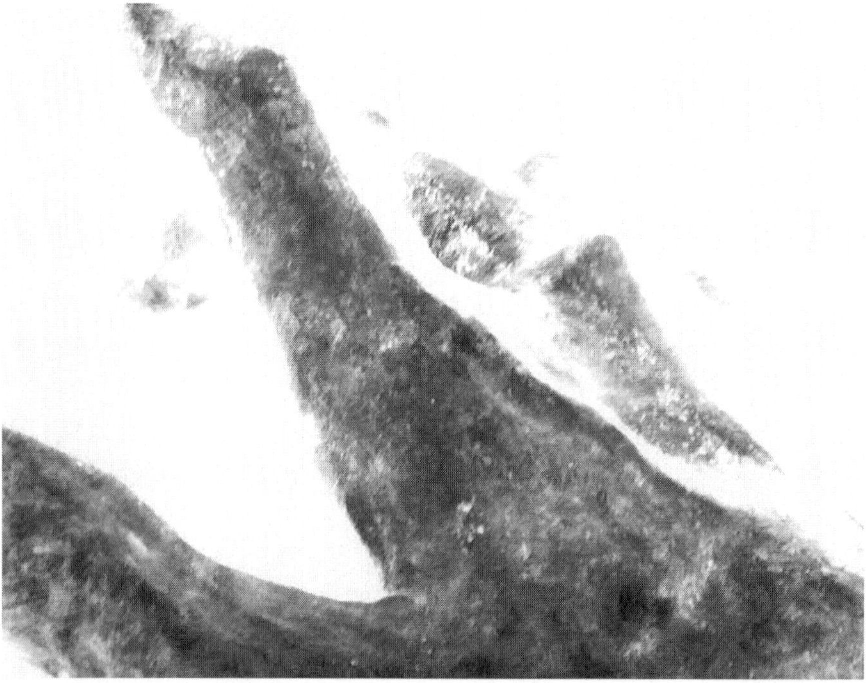

Figure 19. A close-up of the hands of one of the figures from *The Burghers of Calais,* rendered with overexposure effects. Still from *Fragments* (2011).

other, can assume the function of an apparatus, reflecting both its greatness and its misery. The hand is portrayed as a tool that can continually mold new forms while also measuring, cataloging, and sanctioning what exists on the basis of a predetermined principle. It has the power to create, yet it can also grasp, seize, and block. The hand is envisioned as both the subject and object of itself.

At the end of the *Fragments* sequence, George's camera focuses on the back of a hand modeled by Rodin (Figure 19). The black-and-white image loses contrast, shifting toward indeterminacy and the potential of pure light.

CHAPTER 5

SPECTROLOGY OF THE BORDER

Balkan Paths

It is early 2016. Director Maria Kourkouta and poet Niki Giannari are working on a film about the Greek Civil War of the 1940s, shooting some survey images near the Idomeni camp, located on the border between Macedonia and Greece. This takes place just days before the European Union decides to close the Balkan route and then, on March 18, seals an agreement with Turkey to return the migrants who had arrived in Greece.[1] Finding themselves in this situation and actively engaged in the field, Kourkouta and Giannari feel the need to focus on what is unfolding in front of them. Their new idea is to document the living conditions of displaced people, in many cases from areas devastated by civil war, mostly from Syria, the Kurdistan region, Pakistan, and Afghanistan.[2] While the two artists investigate the history of Greece, they are confronted with the current plight of migrants. Their decision to tackle such a topical issue would inevitably demand a deep dive into history as well. However, creating a film based on an interval—two periods and events that are not directly linked—would also require engaging with the spatial and temporal complexity inherent in every image.

The notion of a "spectrology of the border," as this chapter is called, is in part an attempt to interpret Kourkouta and Giannari's film by drawing on its title, *Spectres Are Haunting Europe* (*Fantasmata planiountai pano apo tin Europi*, 2016). This title, in turn, refers to the opening sentence of Karl Marx's and Friederich Engels's *The Communist Manifesto*.[3] As discussed in previous chapters, borderlands are increasingly subject to control technologies.

In this context, the cinematographic gaze further aspires to an enhanced vision, which reveals aspects unapparent to the naked eye. This phenomenon, which I will describe as the spectrality of the border mediascape, creates an environment that is simultaneously visible and invisible, dense and multilayered.

Using *Spectres Are Haunting Europe* as a case study and drawing inspiration from its theoretical approach—a film that explores "something like the transcendental coordinates of the migratory experience"[4]—this chapter examines the border in both abstract and concrete terms, framing it through the notions of space, movement, and time.

Following the film's own three-chapter structure, the next section focuses on migration as movement. I analyze the compositional choices adopted by the directors and advance the hypothesis that the film's gaze functions as a "spectrography" of the border, an investigation of movement and stasis. In the following pages we will delve into how the film seems to focus on a cornerstone of Western philosophy. This key tenet, which remains crucial for contemplating contemporary boundaries, is the idea that "movement and stasis, continuity and discreteness are . . . not opposed. They are two aspects or ways of describing the same *process* or flow of matter."[5] The third section brings into focus the forced stop and explores the political potential inherent in this state of stasis. My references to the film are intended to demonstrate how a forcible arrest creates a meeting between individuals from many parts of the world, who, despite having different paths, share largely similar personal and political goals. In the last section, following the narrative evolution of the film, my reflection on movement and stasis expands to geography and history. Jacques Derrida's reflections on Marx and Engels—in a book perhaps also alluded to by the film's title—suggest that discussing spectrality inevitably involves rethinking the relationships between the present and the past, between the journeys of contemporary migrants and the traumas that have shaken the European continent in recent centuries.[6] This is the point where spectrography explicitly transforms into a spectrology of borders.

Crossing (Spectrography #1)

Spectres Are Haunting Europe could aptly be described as the film with the most entries and exits in the history of cinema. The opening shot reveals a barren terrain, cut in two by a muddy lane. For several minutes the camera remains motionless as hundreds of people cross the field from right to left and left to right. They wear work clothing, outdoor gear, and hiking boots. They push luggage, strollers, and baby carriages (Figure 20). When montage comes into play, the compositional choices in the film's first chapter stay mostly the same. Even as the framing shifts to capture the oblique angles of the refugee camp's terrain and emergency architecture, the film's edges are repeatedly crossed and recrossed. In contrast, the soundtrack captures atmospheric noises, enhancing a sense of presence and serving to ensure the continuity of a natural and social environment beyond the margins of each shot.

A sudden and repeated stepping into and out of the frame is something of a rarity in cinema history. Whether in fiction or documentary, individuals who expose themselves to the camera's eye, allowing themselves to become visible, typically do so to play a role or perform an action, with the aim of expressing an emotion, drive, or perception that is clearly recognizable. When someone repeatedly enters and exits a frame, it highlights the fact that we are watching a film, adding a theoretical and critical dimension to the viewing experience. In these moments, the film reflects on itself as a medium, based on the construction of a space—the relationship between what is visible on-screen and what is perceived off-screen—and on the reproduction of movement from movement itself. To start, we might ask: What possible models, explicit or implicit, influenced the unusual compositional choices in *Spectres Are Haunting Europe*? What does the first part of the film convey about the border and its crossing? More importantly, what relationship is established between the limits of cinematographic space and the border, understood as a geopolitical issue?

A closer look reveals that all these entrances and exits are unrelated to the stage dynamics rooted in classical theater. Traditionally,

Figure 20. Migrants walking along a flat path cross the cinematic frame—a recurring visual motif that can be read as a reflection on the idea of movement. Still from *Spectres Are Haunting Europe* (2016).

the relationships between *skenè* (scene), *proskenion* (proscenium), and *parodoi* (side entrances)—which allow characters to enter and exit the stage, simulating departures and arrivals to other narrated locations—create a spectacular conception of space. This is based both on what is directly visible to the spectators and on what they are prompted to imagine as contiguous.[7] According to this conception, entry and exit are guided by a principle of "economy" *(oikonomia)*, which aligns with narrative needs and dramaturgical choices, based on a specific vision of what a show should be and the effect it should have on viewers. In contrast, Kourkouta and Giannari's film systematically questions this principle of narrative economy and its corresponding effect. Here, people traverse the frame continuously, without even stopping in front of the camera, leaving no room for them to play a dramatic role. Those we see in this film are *passeurs* through a space that is at once filmic and geopolitical.

In the face of this incessant flow along the horizontal axis, even a nod to the compositional model of ancient Greek pottery—

where figures arranged in profile create an effect of narrative objectivity—becomes impossible. In that model, figures appeared to look at each other, a rhetorical strategy for depicting mythological and historical deeds.[8] Conversely, in the first part of *Spectres Are Haunting Europe,* no border crosser stands out from the others as a hero or a leader. This stream of walkers seems to lack both a beginning and an end, with no clear single direction of movement: some go to the left, others to the right; or perhaps they are the same individuals going back and forth?

Despite a superficial similarity, the profile figures in this film cannot be associated with the famous experiments in motion photography developed by Eadweard Muybridge in the late nineteenth century either. Like the *Animal Locomotion* series (1872–85), which explored the gestures and movements of humans and other animals, *Spectres Are Haunting Europe* also focuses explicitly on the progression of the human body as it moves across the horizontal plane.[9] Other experimental films made by Maria Kourkouta, such as the series *10 Subway Preludes* (2008–12), also show an interest in the breakdown of movement. Yet, in Muybridge's image series, the human or animal subject occupies the center of the frame. It serves as an example that stands for a type, defined by speciesism, gender identity, or other criteria. Muybridge concentrated on photographically breaking down the gestural forms that make up a movement, which, from his point of view, define a man as a man, a woman as a woman, and so on. In contrast, Kourkouta and Giannari's film goes far beyond such notions of species and gender; the shots in the first part do not follow the subject's movements.[10] Their aim is not to dissect movements and gestures into minimal units. Rather than focusing on a single emblematic or paradigmatic subject that is framed and scanned, the film presents a cluster and a multitude in transit. This compositional choice gives rise to an original reflection on the relations between impersonal movement, the diegetic space of the film, and the geopolitical space of the border.

Instead of framing the actor's or character's appearance to encourage viewer identification with a protagonist's gestures, or breaking down the gestures of an individual subject identified as a type, the first chapter of the film presents migration as a beam of energy that disrupts the shot. *Spectres Are Haunting Europe* provides a "spectrography," revealing movement itself and rendering all borders provisional and relative. The film conveys a Bergsonian and Deleuzian idea of cinema, where image and movement coincide instead of simply animating individual static poses. Cinema, writes Gilles Deleuze, "does not give us an image to which movement is added, it immediately gives us a movement-image. It does give us a section, but a section which is mobile, not an immobile section + abstract movement."[11] From this perspective, Kourkouta and Giannari's film is not merely a documentation of what is happening along the Greek–Macedonian border; it is a cinematic reflection on the notions of movement and becoming.

A recurring theme in previous chapters of this book is that borders are constructed in many ways. They rely equally on static, immovable technologies and portable ones. Political borders do not simply coincide with the sharp dividing lines of a frontier; they extend into space through border mediascaping. As emphasized in the first, third, and fourth chapters, borders are hooked into migrants through biometric tools, personalizing frontiers and creating an overlap between geopolitics and biopolitics. These technologies produce a cast of individual traits, breaking down the body's dynamism into a series of static poses. They then use this cast to assert their ability to detect and control a subject, disregarding the inherently dynamic nature—both spatially and temporally—of any subjectivity, whether individual or social. It is as if these biopolitical and geopolitical technologies, in their quest to contain the potential of movement, resort to Zeno's paradox of Achilles and the tortoise. As we know, this paradox argues that Achilles, the fastest man in the world, can never catch up with a tortoise that starts a race several yards ahead of him. By the time Achilles reaches the tortoise's starting point (A1), the tortoise will have traveled a small distance (T0-T1). When Achilles covers this stretch (A1-A2), the tortoise will have advanced further (T1-T2), and so on. Aristotle's *Physics* contains discussion and refutation of this paradox: "in a race the quickest runner can never overtake the slowest, since the pursuer must first reach the point whence the pursued started, so that the slower must always hold a lead. . . . And the axiom that which holds a lead is never overtaken is false: it is not overtaken, it is true, while it holds a lead: but it is overtaken nevertheless if it is granted that it traverses the finite distance prescribed."[12]

The central issue in both the philosophical debate between the fifth and fourth centuries BCE and modern discussion on the functioning of contemporary borders is the question of movement. Some argue that Achilles (or the migrant) is condemned to being perpetually one step behind the tortoise, who started slightly earlier and whose position corresponds to the space beyond the frontier. Others choose to focus on the reasons for movement, asserting that it cannot be reconstructed through static poses or posthumous reconstructions of the subjects' dynamism.

Unlike border management technologies, which resemble Zeno's paradox by making casts of bodies or stopping movement and slowing it down in a series of poses to allow the border to inch forward, the film by Kourkouta and Giannari generates image-movement itself. Much like a study on migrant and border theory yet resembling a description of *Spectres Are Haunting Europe,* "the image is the moving process through which matter twists, folds and is reflected in various structures of sensation. The migrant is also defined by its flows, folds and circularities, always in transit and trapped between worlds."[13]

Migrants move as often from left to right as from right to left, equally in both directions. The border is also a place of deceleration and disorientation. As the first chapter of the film progresses, the composition of the shots emphasizes the railroad tracks that guide the migrants' path. At a certain point, the flow slows down. We then see, in a detailed close-up, the feet of the migrants lined up in single file, one behind the other. The tracks become a balance beam amidst a sea of mud, where the steps of the people in motion exhibit the choreographic nature of everyday actions—particularly the most challenging ones that typically arise in emergencies. We have reached the impasse of the frontier. There is no more crossing. Where movement is halted, migrants can only hope to achieve their goal by threatening to disrupt all other flows: they must block the train.

Stopover (Spectrography #2)

After a fade to black, both the entrances and the exits dwindle, marking the start of the film's second chapter. The camera now frames groups of migrants gathered near the railroad tracks. They hold signs written in different languages: "Some families sold everything to arrive here. Open the border!" "Bitte. Helfen Sie mir damit kann ich mein kind sehen. Bitteeeeee" (Please. Help me so I can see my child. Pleeeeeeeeease), and so forth. There is a sudden shift from the visual regime of "profile" to that of "frontality." The directors adopt medium full shots, as if to focus on social dynamics within the group of migrants and to dilate the temporality of the narration (Figure 21).

Unlike television images chronicling the "European Migrant Crisis" or the images in a film like Ai Weiwei's *Human Flow* (2017)—dominated by drone ascents and descents framing rows of people from above[14]—the experimental character of a film like *Spectres Are Haunting Europe,* which alternates between rigorous compositional choices, is essential for documenting what is happening at borders. While the arrangement of figures in profile expresses the idea of the image—and migration—as a long-lasting movement, the frontal positioning of bodies and faces serves a different political purpose, creating an intersubjective space that engages and challenges viewers.[15] In the first chapter of the film, the composition of space is centrifugal—migrants move out of the frame. In the second chapter, the film shifts to a centripetal composition—inviting viewers to come closer or inside and gain a sense of the complex political character of each assembly.[16]

We observe the emergence of possible leaders within the forced stopover area, as well as the needs and desires of those trapped between Greece and Macedonia, looking northward. At a certain point, as a crowd gathers along the tracks, we witness a heated confrontation over migration, encapsulating the public debate that has engulfed an entire continent. The forced stopover experience transforms into a moment of encounter and discussion on European public ground. Furthermore, the forced stopover becomes an opportunity for political struggle, challenging the strategic arrangement of the border mediascape—and thus the deter-

Figure 21. Migrants holding signs pleading for help and recognition enact an assembly in the border zone. Still from *Spectres Are Haunting Europe* (2016).

mination of who has the right to move or stand on public land. This gesture is laden with implications that prompt us to critically reflect on the widespread ignorance of the European public regarding border management technologies, an ignorance that results in a generalized lack of interest, vigilance, and militancy about the problematic design of huge geographical areas.

As Judith Butler wrote in a book intended to connect distinct and distant fields of struggle,

> when bodies assemble on the street, in the square, or in other forms of public space (including virtual ones) they are exercising a plural and performative right to appear, one that asserts and instates the body in the midst of the political field, and which, in its expressive and signifying function, delivers a bodily demand for a more livable set of economic, social, and political conditions no longer afflicted by induced forms of precarity.[17]

Butler then remarks on the risk that the media runs of spectacularizing and thus downplaying the political potential of assembly in public space. This issue is particularly significant when considering borders as media and spectacular environments. Butler also emphasizes the need to find solutions to this problem, such as fostering reciprocity between the living forms of assembly and their media representation in today's world.[18]

Spectres Are Haunting Europe embraces these issues, measuring itself against the quality of the initiatives in border areas and seeking to extend and bolster them through its expressive language. In doing so, the film contributes to the revitalization of the Balkan border mediascape with an emphasis on openness and restoring the migrants and their agency. Their enforced temporary stop becomes an opportunity to regenerate the European public sphere, by encouraging thought about the continent's present condition and fostering concern about what is happening at both its center and peripheries. By foregrounding the stopover, the film invites a critical reassessment of how mobility and immobility are structured and experienced. It draws our attention to these states of suspension, revealing them as politically charged situations in which authority is exercised, resistance emerges, and new forms of collective identity begin to take shape. The stopover is reimagined here as a form of dialectical engagement, negotiation, and potential political transformation. In other words, openness should not be understood solely in extensive terms—as the ability to move through the territory—but also in intensive terms, as the ways in which space is inhabited and how that inhabitation shapes the political character of the public realm.

Interval (Spectrology)

The last fifteen minutes—the film's third chapter—stand apart from what we have seen so far. "You were right. / Men will forget these trains / as they forget those. / But the ashes / remember." While images of refugees appear on-screen, Lena Platonos's voice-over begins reciting Niki Giannari's poem "Spectres Are Haunting Europe: Letter from Idomeni" ("Des spectres hantent l'Europe: Lettre de Idomeni"). This time, the images are in black and white, shot on 16-millimeter film, and appear faded like historical documents (Figure 22). But who are these people? And, more impor-

Figure 22. Black-and-white 16-millimeter shot showing a line of migrants with tents behind, while a voice-over suggests an "anachronistic" and "anatopistic" view of migration. Still from *Spectres Are Haunting Europe* (2016).

tantly, where did these men and women and their children come from, and when? Could they be the same individuals we encountered in the previous chapters of *Spectres Are Haunting Europe*? If so, why are they now filmed in black and white, as if in footage from the past? Are they perhaps migrants, fleeing one of the many catastrophes of the twentieth century?

After a few seconds, viewers can easily recognize that these images depict the same contemporary event shown in the previous chapters of the film. However, the change in format and the black-and-white tones signal that something has changed. Here, the film invites us to ponder the complexity of images, highlighting the simple fact that, when faced with an event, film frames bifurcate "in two dissymmetrical jets, one of which makes all the present pass on, while the other preserves all the past."[19] In simpler terms, it is as if each frame were split in two: one part offers the transparency of representation, fulfilling the need to share information, while the other part embodies the opacity of the trace, determining the conditions for these images' archivability and their potential to endure in future historical contexts, with varying degrees of ghostliness.

We encountered this at the start of this chapter. Originally, the directors intended to make a film about war events, deportations, and migrations during the Greek Civil War of the 1940s. Ultimately, they ended up making a film about the Balkan route during the second decade of the twenty-first century. Despite the two distinct historical contexts, the film invites us to contemplate how certain geographic areas are palimpsests of traumatic histories. The paths taken by contemporary migrants have already been traveled by other migrants before them. The need to rethink contemporary frontiers from an archaeological perspective is a recurring theme. In addition to the films shot in Calais, Vallorbe, and Lampedusa analyzed earlier in this book, I will mention *The Milky Way: Nobody Saves Himself on His Own* (*The Milky Way: Nessuno si salva da solo,* 2020) and *The Western Border* (*Il confine occidentale,* 2018) by Luigi D'Alife. This account combines the documentation of present-day conditions under which contemporary migrants attempt to cross the Alps while avoiding border police with early-twentieth-century records of the precarious conditions Italian migrants, mainly from southern Italy, faced in their attempts to arrive in France. The films illustrate that the traumatic and repressed past of European citizens is not far removed from the current realities of others. Conversely, today's non-European migrants can be imagined as a return or visitation by those Europeans who were scattered and displaced during the early-twentieth-century upheavals.

In a book devoted to *Spectres Are Haunting Europe,* which opens with Niki Giannari's poem mentioned earlier, Georges Didi-Huberman writes:

> After all, refugees do nothing but return *[revenir]*. They do not "land" from nothing or nowhere. When we think of them as a crowd of invaders who have come in hostility, when we confuse the enemy with the foreigner, this means that we are trying to avert something that has in fact already taken place: something that you repress from your genealogy. This thing is that we are all children of migrants and that migrants are

> nothing more than our undead relatives *[parents revenants]*, when they are even "distant."[20]

This insight—that the migrants flocking to the continent's borders are none other than the relatives of the people who already live in Europe—leads Didi-Huberman to develop his argument along two main lines. First, he revisits Aby Warburg's thought, emphasizing the inseparable connection between images and migration across both space and time.[21] Second, he underscores the need to revisit the concept of montage as a critical method, a recurring theme throughout his work. Critically examining political borders requires a unified grasp of history and geography. These elements are mutually imbricated: contemporary geopolitical arrangements are rooted in violent military and colonial histories, while the migrants' border crossings expose and reveal traumatic legacies and their impact on the present.[22]

"The camps of today are not the camps of yesterday," Didi-Huberman writes a little later, referring to Nazi extermination and the contemporary system of political border management, "but they are still camps, that is, places where little is needed for injustice to be organized: their very structure is the fruit of an already long history. A history that, without the states getting too worried, had begun through 'simple' retention procedures."[23] In this passage, he considers the moral permissibility and political potential of creating juxtapositions between distinct and distant events through images that remain or refer to them. The theme of anachronism emerges here, along with what I propose to term "anatopism": distant moments and different places not strictly connected by a cause and effect, with the aim of highlighting both differences and recurring features. This approach seeks to connect forms of control and spaces of detention for stateless, displaced, or precarious individuals, established at different times and places, to identify paradigmatic aspects.

While the first two chapters of Kourkouta and Giannari's film focus on the movements and stases of the migrants, providing a kind of *spectrography* of the border, the third chapter explicitly delves into the stratification of space and time, transforming the cinematographic investigation into a form of *spectrology*.

Contemporary Europe is reached or crossed by migrants from other continents. However, Europe is also haunted by ghostly apparitions from its mid- and long-term history of fratricidal wars, feelings of revanchism, opposing blocs, displaced populations, and a colonial past that tends to be reproduced in the frameworks of migration emergencies and their governance.

Specters are roaming contemporary Europe: they are the migrants we see in daily media reports. We must deconstruct the journalistic and media rhetoric that either portrays migrants as threats or renders them invisible, turning them into ghosts. However, the connection between migration and ghosts is far deeper and more problematic than any media portrayal. It relates to the legacies of the past and the ongoing shipwrecks of the present.[24] The specters presented by Kourkouta and Giannari need to be taken seriously. It is not the migrants who are specters or made into specters by the media; rather, through their crossings and encampments, migrants expose the spectral and violent nature of European history and geography. While Marx and Engels sought to starkly contrast "this nursery tale of the Spectre of Communism with a manifesto of the party itself,"[25] Kourkouta and Giannari argue that it is impossible to dismiss specters as "fables" or to effectively drive them out by opposing them with simple facts. Every political claim must be framed within a large reference horizon. It is the task of those engaged in the arts and aesthetics to ensure that the revolutionary and innovative impulses of the present continue to illuminate and enrich our understanding of past events, and vice versa.

Those who work with moving images are not tasked with learning how "to make conversation with the ghost but how to talk with him, with her, how to let them speak or how to give them back speech, even if it is in oneself, in the other, in the other in oneself they are always *there,* specters, even if they do not exist, even if they are no longer, even if they are not yet."[26] We already explored this in previous chapters, especially when addressing the traces of the past and their application in the present. This involves the phantasmatic nature linked to the traumatic events they refer to, the effort to use them in the pursuit and assertion of truth, and ultimately, the need for their narrative reconfiguration. Like Derrida in *Specters of Marx,* the directors of *Spectres Are Haunting Europe* aim to develop a spectrology, contributing to new forms of awareness about migration and, consequently, new forms of recognition. The film's most interesting and original insight is that the spectral nature of migration should not be dismissed as mere fiction but embraced and reimagined positively. The ghostly images appearing on screens in border areas should not provoke forms of rejection or suppression; instead, they should make us aware that the migrants' footsteps and crossings open wide the hinges of history and time. In this way they reaffirm an open and dynamic notion of geography.

The film is a spectrography and spectrology of the border because it views diaspora—from a Greek word meaning "disseminate"—as a recurring feature. The images in the final chapter of *Spectres Are Haunting Europe,* suspended between different times, are an invitation to question the logic governing the continent's edges and to see politics, history, and geography as a unified field of inquiry and an integrated approach to understanding our reality.

CHAPTER 6

PARTICIPATION AND CITIZENSHIP

Migrants and Movie Cameras

A recurring issue, and one that will inevitably appear again both inside and outside of this book, is the paradoxical centrality of geographical borders and social margins. Over the decades, the living conditions of the marginalized and excluded have captured the interest of historians, novelists, journalists, and filmmakers, as well as anyone who is committed to the function of witnessing. However, those who discuss the "margin" often do so *from* a "center" and *for* other centers. They use a language (or languages) that frequently fails to align with or challenge the expressive forms typical of the context in question. At most, they take up some of their aspects—appropriating gestures, postures, or slang expressions—and merely emphasize them. These issues were already pivotal in Antonio Gramsci's thought, in the early twentieth century, and thus also appear in pioneering research in cultural and postcolonial studies.[1]

In previous chapters I detailed the geographic coordinates and contingencies under which the various films were made. In many cases, a space of aesthetic cooperation between subjects of different backgrounds and in different conditions has emerged. In some films, the migrants' ability to document the stages of their journey joins with the production and distribution resources of European filmmakers. In other cases there is a collaborative relationship between the gazes of European filmmakers and those living in refugee camps, between the cinematic apparatus and the migrants' agency, alongside their tactics of resistance. This chapter explores participatory films in contexts involving migrants and so-called second- or third-generation individuals.

Over the past few decades, the ideas of "creation" and "participation" have been conceptualized together, with two objectives: first, to emphasize the social aspect and collective nature of all artistic processes, moving beyond the inclination to credit the final work to a single author; and second, to reinforce a notion of artistic and media practice as a means of political and social engagement.[2] This issue has become particularly relevant in reference to the condition of those who find themselves living in a country other than their country of birth, at risk of discrimination and marginalization. As has been noted, "as active narrators of their stories on social media and as participants on networked commons that make claims to the city and its resources, migrants regularly participate in urban infrastructures of welfare, contest their containment within stereotypical binaries, and open up their own space for individual creativity and political agency."[3]

By focusing on audiovisual projects developed by the ZaLab association in Italy, I aim to reflect on participatory practice from a historical and theoretical perspective. This approach seeks to reveal the implicit aspects of participatory practice in general, and specifically those of the workshops conducted by the association. ZaLab is a cultural laboratory dedicated to producing and distributing free, independent, and socially conscious cinema. Since its founding in the early 2000s, it has produced and distributed documentaries on migratory phenomena in the Mediterranean. These include *Limbo* (2014) by Matteo Calore and Gustav Hofer, *Closed Sea* (*Mare chiuso,* 2012) by Andrea Segre and Stefano Liberti, *Green Blood* (*Il sangue verde,* 2010) by Andrea Segre, *Our Best Years* (*I nostri anni migliori,* 2011) by Stefano Collizzolli and Matteo Calore, and *Like a Man on Earth* (*Come un uomo sulla terra,* 2008) by Andrea Segre, Dagmawi Yimer, and Riccardo Biadene, among many others. Over the years, ZaLab has conducted participatory film workshops in the Tunisian desert, on the West Bank, on the outskirts of Barcelona, and with asylum seekers in Bologna and Rome. They have also worked with second-generation youth in Padua and

Italian migrants in Australia. Additionally, some projects have been developed within the System for the Protection of Asylum Seekers and Refugees (SPRAR), taking place in border facilities like those discussed in previous chapters.[4]

The second section of this chapter adopts a genealogical approach to examining the teachings of Cesare Zavattini, a master of Italian neorealism and the inspiration behind ZaLab. According to the association's web page on participatory video theory, "we chose the name in homage to our master ('Za' from Zavattini, 'Lab' from laboratories), who dedicated his research to experimentation in the context of a social process of 'free' video production. This is a cinema, a television, and a web diffusion that are born from the participatory process of collective elaboration of micro-stories of everyday life by unaccredited eyes, what is called 'Participatory Video.'"[5] My goal is to synthesize aspects of Zavattini's theory of participatory film and assess his legacy up to the present. The third section focuses on a specific ZaLab production, *Flying Roots* (2019), made under the supervision of Michele Aiello and Davide Crudetti by the young participants in a workshop. The film is set in Rome's Piazza Vittorio Emanuele II, an area known for its intercultural interactions and the ongoing transformation of its urban landscape. I did not choose this film because of its artistic merit. Rather, my interest in *Flying Roots* stems from its exploration of the intersection between "native born" individuals and "digital natives," as well as its focus on using both old and new media technologies as tools for expression and recognition. I will begin with *Flying Roots* and then broaden the discourse by including other films produced within workshops or through participatory practices. This serves to chronicle forms of life in the metropolitan periphery and to reference migrants' journeys across the European continent. The fourth section examines the practices and aesthetics that characterize participatory audiovisual production as a form of social and political action. This approach results in a concept of urban space, whether central or marginal, that becomes livable through the continuous writing and rewriting of narratives that interweave the stories of its residents.

New and Old Frontiers of Participatory Cinema

In a study devoted to the margins of twentieth-century Italy, the historian David Forgacs draws attention to the

> risk for anyone who "takes up the cause" of the marginalized, namely that the act itself of denouncing these people's conditions, and the belief that one can thereby move them "from margins to centre," may serve as a palliative or a catharsis, both for the person doing the denouncing and for his or her implied audience, and this can prevent them from identifying what actually produces that condition: economic inequality, laws, policies, prejudices.[6]

In his book, Forgacs refers to Pier Paolo Pasolini and Carlo Levi as examples of intellectuals whose work and gaze are fixed on the peripheries of progress. In contrast, I want to highlight another Italian artist and theorist whose vision of cinema, the visual arts, and literature offers insights into the paradox of the margin's centrality. Cesare Zavattini, a writer and public intellectual, is often recognized as the story author and screenwriter of classics such as *Shoeshine* (*Sciuscià*, 1946), *Bicycle Thieves* (*Ladri di biciclette,* 1948), and *Miracle in Milan* (*Miracolo a Milano,* 1951), or as a utopian dreamer known for his militant reflections on art and society. It is important to look beyond a rigid opposition between practice and theory in Zavattini's writings, as he created a series of concepts, tools, and keys for understanding the present, media invasiveness, and social and political margins.[7]

Zavattini's theoretical teachings, centered on the relationship between media, society, and participation, can be organized around three nodes. The first is the democratization of media, which occurs through the spread of technologies. However, it also requires acknowledging the proximity between the skills and actions of artistic workers and factory or other production sector workers. The second node develops a non-logocentric concept of reading and writing, articulated through audiovisual forms of expression. The third reassembles the relationship between media and everyday life, where media participation is seen as a shared existence within the same social world or common environment.

The idea of a possible technological democratization is conceived by Zavattini in relation to the condition of subalternity, going beyond the limits of a purely utopian vision.[8] In a book investigating his theoretical and artistic stature, Stefania Parigi notes that

> technological globalization, which he saw looming on the horizon, seems to have brought many of its tensions to fruition, but completely corroding—as is obvious—the moral paradigm on which they were founded. The search for the true and the immediate, the counter-information, the constant questioning of the world, the emergence of the artistic subjectivity of each individual on the web, the dialogue and interdependence of cultures and experiences are all elements that emerge in a space of apparent democratization of communication and that are simultaneously reabsorbed into the noise of media simulation.[9]

Zavattini's thought does indeed arise from a form of enthusiasm for the potential represented by the widespread diffusion of technologies in mid-twentieth-century Italy, coupled with the questioning of their use conditions. In an unpublished text from the mid-1940s, he writes that "the most modest individual has his own small telephone and television set, which he wears on his arm like a watch, by means of which he can talk to whomever he wants and see events from hour to hour under any latitude and longitude."[10] This prophetic and detailed description of a "smartwatch" could be seen as a form of clairvoyance, underscoring his surprising ability to be a major player in the film industry while pushing the imagination beyond the boundaries of his historical time.

Nevertheless, in the late 1960s, during the era of *cinegiornali liberi* (free newsreels), his political commitment became even more explicit.[11] Zavattini never wavered in making the need to overcome the production mechanisms that tie cinema to capitalistic production systems and the specific skills of the workers central to critical and political debate. In a letter dated 1969, he wrote:

> We ask the periphery, the base or grassroots, to name events, provide data. This will help to carry out a more focused critique. They'll provide plans for shooting sequences, acting on

> our request, but also select earlier footage, which was never used, or was badly used, since we aim to draw a substantial, live, map for Italians to see, making good cinematic use of whatever is available in film archives and whatever is happening in the real world. . . . The Centre needs to be more active than it is. It needs to be inventive, even to the point of constantly contradicting its own frames of analysis, as and when the frames come into contact with the reality of the moment.[12]

In the same document, he argues vigorously and consistently that "We're not making a film, but making a revolutionary intervention prior to making the film, while we are making the film, and after we've made the film. . . . This type of cinema is really flexible to editing and re-editing, with the inclusion of new footage, determined by input from the periphery, by events, and by unimaginable circumstances arising during the struggle."[13] Here, the notion of editing or assemblage links the realms of moving images and manufacturing so strongly that it rethinks and reconfigures their relations. In Italy during the second half of the twentieth-century, the opposition between center and margin and the divide between intellectuals and subalterns could be challenged by recognizing and exploring the relationship between the tools and production practices of the cinematic apparatus and those used in the primary and secondary sectors. In other words, the camera, tripod, and lights are also "tools" that require no more or less skill than those of a field worker, carpenter, welder, or tailor—thus enabling their appropriation to express a look, culture, and form of action.

Starting in the 1930s and 1940s, Zavattini explored the renewed idea of "writing," moving seamlessly from literature to painting and investigating the boundaries between these forms of expression. In a sense, he felt free to transcend them to achieve an expanded, experimental concept of languages.[14] During this period he also took an explicit stance on filmmaking: "One day we will use the film camera as we use the pen and the brush today."[15] Similarly, in later decades, writing in the pages of *Cinema Nuovo,* Zavattini proposed a new form of teaching and learning: "No one has ever thought of setting a school essay to be done using a camera. If that happened, teaching would be required to be more relevant to reality and teachers themselves required to become proficient in using a camera."[16] With this statement, he demonstrated a precocious understanding that a new writing technique beyond pen and paper was now possible. As he stressed here, thanks in part to the camera, cognitive and critical processes could be activated starting from primary school, with multiple implications for social life. The originality of his insight lies not just in his foresight, anticipating Alexandre Astruc's idea of *caméra-stylo,* the concept of using the camera as a pen.[17] Most striking is Zavattini's notion of writing as an expressive form that is not only verbal but also pictorial, graphic, photographic, and cinematographic. Most importantly, he disassociated the idea of writing from individual authorship, opening it up to a participatory notion. This idea was also present in Dziga Vertov's Kino-Eye theory and practice.[18]

Writing with images does not mean subordinating all forms of expression to the literary; instead, it seeks to break free from its hegemony. Writing with cinema involves recognizing that screens, as enablers of techno-aesthetic mediation, are spaces where psychological, gestural, and social flows are inscribed continuously. In this sense, rather than simply proving that one has "acquired a language" or has "a beautiful calligraphy," writing with visual media is a performative gesture, much like the artistic avant-garde from the 1920s to the 1960s and later.[19] Just as neorealism went beyond merely telling stories of poverty and marginalization, by renewing the cinematic language, the political force of Zavattini's thought lay not just in focusing on the excluded or on organizing schools of participatory cinema in the suburbs of Rome or Milan.[20] Participatory cinema, associated with the spread of technology, is filled with risks and potential, but more importantly, it demands that we go beyond a preconceived, spectacular idea of the cinematographic *mise-en-scène.* This shift allows us to value the spatial condition of encounters and the temporal condition of becoming, a process that remains open-ended.[21]

In the 1970s, in answer to a series of interview questions, Zavattini summarized his enthusiasm for the expressive potential of audiovisual media. With cinema, he stated, "for the first time the instrument became incorporated into the function of the instrument . . . that is, it was not just a means, it was a synthesis."[22] He went on to point out that "the camera was a medium that put as little space as possible between me and reality, and that literature, on the other hand, made it increasingly difficult to understand."[23] Traditionally, literature is seen as a form of expression based on the logos and codified by a grammar. In contrast, the moving image offers a space to experiment with the concept of apparatus and experience the positive implications of mediation. Zavattini, the greatest screenwriter of neorealist cinema and a profound connoisseur of writing, envisioned a kind of a cinema without cinema. However, caution is required here: the phenomenon Zavattini describes is not a naive conception of realism where the medium is made transparent for the benefit of reality. Rather than denying mediation, Zavattini viewed it as deeply embedded in both individual and collective practices. In contemporary philosophical and media terms, Zavattini investigated continuity and discontinuity between the *medial condition*—the existential condition of "being-in-a-medium"[24]—and the *media condition,* understood as interaction with technological devices.

Although Zavattini's participatory cinema spans from democratization to an expanded notion of writing that includes media practices and forms of everyday life, it is not a codified method. But neither is it a mere utopia. It is a theoretical insight that anticipated our twenty-first-century relationship with media, foreseeing its widespread presence, its intrusiveness, and the way "mediation" has become synonymous with contact, experience, and participation in a shared environment. In this context, Zavattini's most radical political expression seems to align with an open conception of mediation practices. Instead of creating a cinema that depicts a preexisting, self-contained reality, it invites us to recognize the role mediation provides: the continuous creation and re-creation of positions and roles between the narrative's subjects and objects. From this perspective, participation consists in a series of gestures that leave traces, forming a polyphonic and polysensorial story, and ultimately establishing a common ground, a perimeter of meaning, and a public space where one can live and gain recognition.

Figure 23. Interacting with a smartphone in the process of making a participatory film. Still from *Flying Roots* (2019).

Native Born and Digital Native

Flying Roots was filmed in Rome's Esquilino quarter with the participation of young people with family roots from various parts of the world. As explained on the film's web page, Michele Aiello and Davide Crudetti from ZaLab supervised the project. It was developed through a preparation phase and two three-month workshops, each involving two groups of twelve adolescents.[25] During these collaborative sessions, the participants acquired filmmaking skills while continuing to discuss social issues, such as the right to citizenship and political participation. At the end of this long process, the final thirty-seven-minute film interweaves the stories of various young participants from the workshop.

The film opens in Piazza Vittorio Emanuele II, an area marked by migration, multiculturalism, and gentrification over the last twenty years.[26] We see close-ups of Micaela, whose family is from Bolivia, and her best friend. Out of focus in the background, behind the details of their hands, is the garden of the large square, a place for meeting, playing, and enacting the "roots" referred to in the film's title. The dialogue between the two girls revolves around

Figure 24. Filming in Rome's Esquiline neighborhood, navigating the space between multiculturalism and gentrification. Still from *Flying Roots* (2019).

the question of identity, framed as a paradox: being Roman and yet not exclusively Roman; the incompatibility between Italy's blood-based right to citizenship and their personal or family origins from other parts of the world; the tension between the *here,* where the two young women live, and an *elsewhere,* where their distant memories lie. The speaker, holding the cell phone that belongs to one of the two girls—always clutched in her hands and always at the center of the film frame (Figure 23)—plays the songs "Muñeco de lego" by Colombian singer Karol G and "Que va" by Colombian Alex Sensation and Puerto Rican Ozuna, both international reggaeton hits. In the terms of film theory and film practice, the music from the portable device transitions from "visualized sounds," whose source is visible in the shot, to "acousmatic sounds," an effect created by the film's editing.[27] The film's initial part ends with a selfie of the two friends in which the video camera's point of view differs from that of the cell phone, mirroring and framing it.

From this point forward, the video camera maintains an "indirect free" relationship with the rhetoric and aesthetics of digital self-representation, based on interaction and tactile contact

Figure 25. Flipping through the family album in a participatory cinema approach that combines old and new ways of preserving and showing memory. Still from *Flying Roots* (2019).

with bodies.[28] Participatory storytelling is initiated through the connection between the portable technologies—familiar tools for the young participants, which they use habitually to capture and share fragments of their lives—and the film's video camera. Accordingly, over the course of the film we follow the Italian–Chinese Federico, who wanders around the Roman neighborhood as a "man with a camera" (Figure 24). We also accompany Ludovica, who follows the trail of her family's Armenian origins by flipping through a particular display device: the photo album (Figure 25). And finally, we follow Scilla, who, through her voice-over, attempts to weave together the stories of the other protagonists.

Flying Roots undoubtedly finds inspiration in other films made in recent years to explore this part of Rome as a multi-ethnic environment—particularly, Abel Ferrara's *Piazza Vittorio* (2017) and Agostino Ferrente's *The Orchestra of Piazza Vittorio* (*L'orchestra di Piazza Vittorio,* 2006). More explicitly, the aesthetic choices in *Flying Roots* are reminiscent of *Selfie* (2019), one of Ferrente's own films, shot in Naples. Despite the qualitative differences between

Flying Roots, a product of a participatory filmmaking workshop, and *Selfie,* a film that has garnered public and critical acclaim, their comparison offers an aesthetic and political insight that leads back to Zavattini's legacy. Both films utilize digital technologies to engage subjects who are not professional filmmakers. And in line with Zavattini's idea of using the camera during schooling, the two films focus on adolescence as a time of learning, transgression, and experimentation with techniques of personal expression and social interaction. In Ferrente's film, the selfie is seen as a performative gesture, enabling subjects to connect with or detach from their geographical and social environment by becoming an image. This transformation serves as a form of participation or withdrawal from public discourse and visual culture.[29] In *Flying Roots,* the protagonists create selfies, conduct interviews, and document neighborhood life. Their actions—clicking, linking to music videos, sending messages, flipping through the pages of a photo album—are synchronized with gestural rhythms that determine the timing of the film montage.

In a philosophical essay that makes explicit reference to the aesthetics of films like *Selfie,* Pietro Montani describes digital media and their billions of users as embodying a syncretic expressive and interpretative attitude with a scriptural or "archiscritural" character:

> The extended writing practiced on displays is becoming the object of learning and internalization processes. This means that the display form of the screen proves to be the most suitable to implement a sensory revolution similar to that inaugurated, in its time, by phonetic writing and, subsequently, by printing with mobile characters. And to bring back in some respects the audio-visual to the idea of "cinematographic writing" as it was intended by some theorists of the cinema of the origins.[30]

Although Zavattini's theories and ZaLab's participatory workshops are not addressed in Montani's reflection, a fruitful connection can be made. If digital technologies are the most current form of the visual media writing process, which was initiated or at least theorized by cinema, we are left to draw the necessary conclusions. Considering what we have seen in *Flying Roots,* we can easily recognize and value the possible relationship between portable technologies—which anyone can use on a daily basis to engage in public discourse—and the medium of film. On one hand, the fragmentary writings of media users can stimulate and renew the compositional processes of cinema, fostering participation and critical reflection. On the other, the history of cinema and filmic forms offers an archive of solutions from which we can draw inspiration to craft images of the present.

In other words, *Selfie* and *Flying Roots* create a connection between the activities of documentation, storytelling, and image sharing, which characterize both new media practices and the audiovisual language and narration that, for almost 150 years now, has been known as "cinematography." These kinds of films also reveal the political nature of an activity that we tend to overlook: the importance of collecting and preserving this content through audiovisual practices that rearticulate the relationships between private and public, personal and social, and local and global. In the realm of digital practice and social media, individuals produce and share vast amounts of images and information, which are increasingly captured by institutional discourses or processed by algorithms and exploited by private corporations. This fragmented and dislocated content can only gain a political function through interconnection processes that counteract fragmentation and reconfigure it through participation, even across historical and geographical boundaries.

In Ferrente's *Selfie,* the two protagonists imagine and capture their own images in different ways, sometimes leading to disagreement. The responsibility of creating a synthesis consequently falls to the director. A similar situation occurs in *Flying Roots,* where the young participants' work is not questioned, yet Aiello and Crudetti's coordinating function remains, appearing explicitly in the project's credits. While the individual protagonists—both in the film and the workshop—independently produce multiple media fragments using their personal devices, the cinematographic work of collecting and reorganizing these fragments requires collegiality and negotiation among different roles. The idea of "participation" should therefore be understood in a broad sense: as a simultaneous adoption and questioning of the various roles and skills of all workshop participants.

Many of the issues that arise from a film like *Flying Roots* also apply to other works that do not originate from film workshops but are nonetheless shaped by participatory dynamics, such as *We Are Not Together* (2019) by Alex Nezam and *Trieste Is Beautiful at Night* (*Trieste è bella di notte,* 2023) by Andrea Segre, Stefano Collizzolli, and Matteo Calore. The first film documents the living conditions of migrants in Greece, especially in the Moria refugee camp on Lesvos and in Athens, following the closure of European borders in 2016. In this film the narrative is partially taken over by the migrants themselves, using portable technologies and storytelling methods akin to those used today in social networks. The second film, produced by ZaLab, investigates the phenomenon of "informal expulsions," where migrants are prevented from formalizing their asylum claims along the Balkan route on the border between Slovenia and Italy. In this film, migrants' mobile phones serve simultaneously as means of long-distance communication; tools for spatial orientation; ways of measuring time in the short, medium, and long term; and techniques for documenting injuries inflicted by military or paramilitary forces, sometimes for forensic purposes in the long process of seeking asylum. But the mobile phone is also a video camera and a platform for audiovisual production and distribution, capable of narrating and accompanying the intercontinental travel. The images produced in this way by migrants—along with their own editing choices, such as the inclusion of the track "Aatish" by Subodh Su2—are incorporated into the film, where they constitute some of its most powerful and affecting moments (Figure 26).

Spivak's question "Can the subaltern speak?," posed in the introduction to this book, is as difficult to answer affirmatively—once and for all, in a simplistic way—as it is necessary to continue addressing.[31] New power relations are expressed and re-expressed by the media, often unintentionally, even in projects meant to be "participatory." In other words, there is always a risk of reintroducing elements such as an external "conscience," a pivot, a facilitator of the telling, a directorial subjectivity, or an ethnocentric vision of technology into both the process and the outcomes. At

Figure 26. A group of migrants look at a smartphone as it records them, highlighting the importance of self-representation in telling their own journeys. Still from *Trieste Is Beautiful at Night* (2023).

the same time, contemporary participatory filmmaking practices reveal the transformation of traditional roles between director, actor, and extras, prompting a reimagining of the center–margin dynamic. Projects like ZaLab empower those forced into subaltern conditions to film, edit, and share images.[32] By interweaving themes of first-, second-, and third-generation migrants with "digital natives," the *Flying Roots* laboratory revitalizes Zavattini's vision of democratizing technologies, affirming a kind of media writing and expanding and renewing both artistic and political discourse.

Film and Citizenship

Citizenship is central to debate in political studies and is a key battleground in contemporary political struggles.[33] While this book does not aim to reconstruct the debate over citizenship, it intends to show the relationship between technological and aesthetic forms that structure border mediascapes and the quality of political life. By shifting attention from legal definitions of national belonging to the representation and self-representation of individuals with family migration histories, I wish to underscore the need for new aesthetic and political frameworks for rethinking citizenship. In other words, citizenship should not be considered exclusively from the perspective of national and supranational authorities but also in terms of the relationships and recognition that develop within social, cultural, and artistic practices.[34]

In this chapter we have focused on *Flying Roots,* a film that intriguingly links the practice of digital and social media to second- or third-generation migrants. Beyond this case study, it is perhaps no coincidence that several films exploring citizenship in contemporary Italy and Europe have a collective or participatory character. These films often feature images created by migrants themselves using nonprofessional technologies. This observation could certainly extend to films such as *18 Ius soli* (2011) by Fred Kudjo Kuwornu; *Welcome to Italy* (*Benvenuti in Italia,* 2012) by Aluk Amiri, Hamed Dera, Hevi Dilara, Zakaria Mohamed Ali, and Dagmawi Yimer; and *Love Has No Borders* (*L'amour n'a pas de frontière,* 2019), made in a participatory video workshop with asylum seekers within the SPRAR in Palermo. In the film *Natives of the New World* (2018), produced, written, and filmed by the KinoMosaik Collective—a group of migrants camped on the island of Lesvos—the ideas of migration and citizenship are reexamined through the lens of participation.[35]

The literature on participatory filmmaking suggests that the practice assigns greater importance to the process than to the outcome. Its goals are "[t]o develop personal skills in use of video technology. To team up with others who also wish to learn how to use video technology. . . . To interact with teachers who view their role as that of a 'co-learner.' To modify personal behavior and strengthen individual identity,"[36] and so forth. This aspect is central to both Zavattini's theory and ZaLab's activity. However, by generally prioritizing the *process* over the *outcome,* nuances may be lost or different kinds of participatory practices may be seen as indistinguishable. As a careful rereading of Zavattini reveals, his thoughts on sharing, socialization, and politicization are consistently inspired by insights into media technologies, including their expressive potential and capacity to connect or distance people, create environments for shared experiences, provoke debate, and facilitate decision making. How should one interpret the statement, quoted earlier, that with cinema "for the first time the instrument became incorporated into the function of the instrument," if not as an emphasis on questioning the hierarchy between process and outcome, thus experiencing their intertwining? And how can we ignore the fact that a certain idea of participation is always embedded in filmmaking, understood as a form of writing?

Whether filmed in SPRAR facilities, refugee camps, or both geographically peripheral and central urban areas, participatory films are primarily opportunities to use the medium of cinema to question the relationship between *means* and *ends*. Philosophical discussions have mostly examined these concepts in terms of their political significance.[37] However, they also hold considerable importance in Gilbert Simondon's reflections on technical culture—a recurring theme throughout this book. Simondon identifies a tendency to view "the employment of means . . . in the position of minority with respect to the result" and the possibility to undo such imbalance in techno-aesthetic configurations that he calls "self-regulated."[38] Even more explicitly, Simondon offers a brief description of cinema that aligns surprisingly with Zavattini's thinking: cinema is "an activity of men in groups and an activity that implies and provokes representations, feelings, voluntary movements, just as it implies and produces an inter-individual relationship in which the individual intervenes not only as a unit, but also as the bearer of a bundle of meanings, intentions, and tendencies that are actualized in the cinematic situation."[39] At least three consequences can be drawn from this quotation, which ties back to the questions and objectives I set at the beginning of this chapter. The first is that cinematic experimentation—whether productive or aesthetic—allows us to observe and question any technological concepts aimed at imposing predefined roles on bodies and territories. The second is that, in the game of cinema, the various production and diegetic roles result from an open dynamic of interaction, leading to outcomes that cannot be fully anticipated until the fieldwork is completed and the narrative framework is concluded, awaiting the next film, and so on. The third, in a broader sense, is that cinema is not merely an illustration of cultural, social, and political phenomena that precede it. It is a tool for critical understanding, capable of revealing the often hidden operational strategies that govern these phenomena.

Participatory cinema is a practice and a form of expression that develops in a dynamic balance with its associated milieu, involving diverse subjectivities and entities that take part in it and animate it. It offers an opportunity to understand the relationship between means and ends and to assess the social and political potential of that relationship. The goal is no longer to direct production and postproduction toward a single aesthetic and commercial outcome, guided by a principle of narrative and financial economy. This does not imply, however, that the idea of making a film should serve simply as an excuse or opportunity like any other to meet and share an experience. For both workshop coordinators and participants, creating a film becomes a chance to reflect on how relationships between subject and object, and among different social roles, are always determined *in the media* and *through the media*. Throughout the introduction and chapters of this book, I have shown how the unevenness, discrimination, and racialization typical of border mediascapes result from a programmatic regimentation of the mediation process. This is achieved through a strategically programmed distribution of roles, identities, possibilities, and rights. In opposition to this, participatory filmmaking and similar approaches aim to assert the affirmative possibilities of mediation. This potential does not reside primarily in favoring "hot border mediascapes" (which involve greater sensory involvement and more direct contact among participants) or "cold border mediascapes" (which rely on sophisticated technologies that process abstract visualizations and operate at a distance). Instead, the political value of mediascapes is defined by the "thermal" instability and self-reflexivity characteristic of participatory media practices—conditions created by the use of both new and old technologies and the interaction of diverse subjects.

There is a deep connection between the ways migrants are welcomed and captured—put into images—in various media and the social, political, and legal forms of their recognition. This necessitates a continual need for critical attention to the images and discourses produced in border mediascapes or at urban margins.[40] Therefore, terms such as "refugee," "asylum seeker," "first-," "second-," and "third-generation migrant," and so on should be viewed as framing mechanisms destined to obstruct self-determination, participation, and recognition. Films such as Dagmawi Yimer's *Va' pensiero* (2013) and *My New European Life* (2019) by Abou Bakar Sidibé and Moritz Siebert demonstrate how these terms and forms of non-recognition continue well beyond obtaining refugee status or citizenship. Reversing this paradigm also requires establishing a new public discourse and visual culture that questions the center–margin relationship through continuous, participatory practices of "rewriting the urban script."[41]

From Za—Cesare Zavattini's favorite autograph—to ZaLab and beyond, an entire alphabet awaits to be written and rewritten. This task seeks to challenge the technologies of border control, overcome the aporias of social and humanitarian communications, and right the asymmetries of speech and gaze that even the most sensitive discourses and committed works of art risk falling into.

FILMING AT THE BORDER

This book could be regarded as a series of film screenings and discussions about contemporary geopolitical borders. Much like a film club, I have tried to interweave the perspectives of cinephiles with those of readers mainly interested in the films' political and social content. It is the moving images, after all, that attract our attention, inviting us to engage with them, directing our gaze to specific issues, and prompting us to take a position. In this understanding of cinema, the more it focuses inward, reflecting on its own history, techniques, and aesthetics, the more it turns outward to the external world. This means that there is no possibility of documentation without experimenting with technical and expressive forms. But it also suggests that the cinematic gaze can prove invaluable, especially when it comes to observing and understanding the functioning of other technologies and their impact. It is as if cinema—or rather, certain moving images—provides the very ideas and conceptual tools needed to develop a critical reflection on some of the most pressing issues of our time. To conclude, I would like to revisit the outcomes of the various chapters and explicitly address the types of objects we have examined as case studies.

A recurring theme, central to the book, is the idea that to reflect on borders, one should focus on media technologies and the different practices and forms of mediation that characterize specific areas. Rather than viewing media as simply implementing or representing preexisting realities—such as laws, political measures, or walls between two states—we began with media as our starting point. From the introduction, we realized that dealing with the border is not just a matter of reaching a destination. Approaching the border means grappling with the techniques by which a given geographical concept is mapped onto the territory and projected over the environment. It means navigating a series of thresholds and a continuous play of *chiaroscuro:* the lighted field inside the frame and the shadowy off-field outside the frame, where one might seek shelter, a hiding spot, or a temporary escape route. Page after page, we have observed that even when media devices redelineate preexisting frontier lines, they actually end up redefining their form and extension. As noted in chapter 3, when discussing the idea of Fortress Europe, borders can take the form of internment architecture or an invisible system of interconnected points. In both cases, borders ultimately appear as multimedia macro installations with significant effects on a psychological, social, and political level.

Although the rhetoric accompanying the mediatization of public spaces emphasizes the values of security, safety, and welcome, the chapters reveal the discriminatory and violent nature of borderlands. Of course, every encounter, exchange, and contact between different individuals and cultures is based on the persistence of multiple thresholds. However, when infrastructure is managed unilaterally, it leads to the control of territories and the people who inhabit or pass through them, or who aspire to, thus unilaterally determining the forms of interaction. As we saw in chapter 2 especially, regarding the Mediterranean, the more borderlands are operationalized, the more they are portrayed as wildlands, extremely dangerous to cross. Under these conditions, environments such as the sea, slopes, or any terrain are *technologically constructed* as *natural borders* that threaten the lives of those denied the right to cross, due to logistical disparities. This way of conceiving the relationship between media and geography is paradoxical. On the one hand, there is a desire to block the forms of transit and exchange that the environment and its elements might enable. On the other hand, a management system is naturalized, thereby concealing specific choices and accountabilities. In response, migrants are forced to adopt a dual approach. First, as explained in chapter 1, they are required to report their location to the patrolling authorities to facilitate intervention and prevent shipwrecks or other "accidents." From this perspective, those standing outside the border share the desire to integrate into the media system of the continent or country of destination. But before they can join that community, the path is incredibly long. They must first send out an SOS, get noticed, identified, and possibly, after crossing countless material and immaterial borders, be recognized. Moreover, their travel experience often requires hiding from technologies that monitor borders to avoid being registered, interned, and involuntarily repatriated.

I have named this apparatus, which finds apparent mitigation and effective implementation in the technological scenario of the new millennium, the "media color line." Although human rights have been established to protect stateless or otherwise precarious individuals, the concept of protection offered by devices operating in borderlands is often perceived differently. Here, it is not the migrants in transit or those in vulnerable conditions who are safeguarded but rather the asymmetrical relationships that define how the border functions, preserving a system of privileges. When surveillance, identification, and data collection take precedence over mutual recognition, technological tools strip migrants of their prerogatives. As discussed especially in chapter 4, regarding biometric controls over bodies, even after crossing what is formally identified as the frontier, migrants encounter the border in the form of devices that perform an immune function, simultaneously including and excluding them in and from communities recognized as belonging to a certain territory through citizenship. In this situation, migrants are typically excluded from the possibility of equal interaction with those who remain on the other side of the border. Instead, they are included within the scope of control, as objects of a gaze or other sensory system that occupies a hierarchically superior position.

The project on the geopolitics of media developed here is not limited to an idealized conception of borders as spaces for intercultural dialogue, nor to a restrictive one that sees them as mere product of control apparatuses. Instead, we explored the hybrid nature of these environments: simultaneously anthropic and physical, technological and natural, imposed from above and redrawn from below. The first challenge was to think of border areas as having different "media temperatures." The notions of *hot borders* and *cold borders* provide conceptual tools for exploring the perceptions, interactions, and inter-definitions that distinguish these geographical and political spaces. In this regard, we analyzed the different techniques used to monitor and manage geographic space and migrant routes. Most of these governmental procedures and practices are meant to forcibly stabilize relations in advance. Yet we have frequently witnessed the persistence of dynamic recognition forms, even in borderline contexts deeply influenced by power imbalances. The second challenge was to consider that the path of migration coincides with a series of mediation environments, where significant new assemblages emerge. If the border apparatus continually poses obstacles to migrants, the devices with which they are equipped and the forms of mediation they engage in assume a distinctly political value. I am referring primarily to migrants' use of media, where a single device—usually a smartphone—can serve multiple functions: communicating remotely with those at their destination or left behind in their country of origin, sending messages to the relevant authorities, seeking forms of orientation, producing documentation, and more. As we have observed, migrants must also experience the material and elemental character of the territories they cross. In this regard, borders also coincide with living environments where different perspectives and fields of struggle intertwine and revitalize each other. In several chapters, a clear relationship emerged between forms of militancy against the border apparatus and ecocritical approaches, as well as between tactics of resistance and forms of resilience.

Throughout the book, I have consistently used terms such as "strategy" and "tactics" to differentiate between a certain *conception of* and particular *approach to* the border. "Strategy" refers to forms of control and management, while "tactics" refers to the adaptations migrants make during their journeys and their attempts to escape the border apparatus. In the current sense of these words, influenced by their military and marketing uses, tactics are generally considered to follow strategies, both temporally and logically. Contrary to this view, the various chapters suggest a reversal in the relationship between the two notions. The technological implications of border control strategies reveal their largely "reactionary" nature, as they arrive in response to preceding events and consistently lag behind an open social and environmental process. Viewing technology as merely a casting, datafication, or tracking tool overlooks the dynamic character of what it conveys and from which it continually emerges and reemerges.

While control systems are integrated into the daily lives of European and Western citizens, who surrender personal information in exchange for access to several networks and services, the position migrants are put in exposes them to the adverse and violent effects of these apparatuses. This is evident in the attempt to align personal and biometric data with their identity, imposing fixed limits on their conduct and movement within geographic spaces. This point arose in connection with the Dublin Convention, subsequent regulations, and the Eurodac system, which regulate the identification and allocation of asylum seekers to various European states, often against their will. This issue was explored in chapters 2 and 4, focusing on the notion of "trace," and in chapter 5, with reference to Zeno's paradox, which blocks movement by equating it to a series of static poses. In contrast to these strategic limitations, the affirmative nature of tactics is evident in participatory projects, analyzed in chapter 6, which can suspend the subordination of means to ends. Even when the tactics adopted by migrants are extreme, painful, and apparently negative—such as the removal of fingerprints discussed in chapter 4—they always contain an affirmative element. Migrants do more than just traverse spaces and cross borders: they challenge conventional notions of both media and geography. Using a term I have employed throughout the book, their routes, daily practices, and forms of resistance take on an "anatopistic" character: they connect disparate places—such as contemporary European borders and colonial frontiers from the past—revealing continuity within difference. The insight they transmit prompts us to see geography as not fixed but dynamic, shaped by histories and memories. From this awareness, they create the basis for a new vision of border spaces.

The choice to focus on a series of documentary films as case studies allowed us to examine various contexts in Europe in the new millennium: from the Mediterranean Sea, between Libya and Lampedusa, to the Swiss Alps, bordering France and Germany; from Calais to the waters between Turkey and the Greek islands, and to Idomeni. We also considered films made in Melilla, in the Susa Valley, between Italy and France, and in many other areas. The idea of cinema emerging from this book is that of a geographical and social machine, capable of performing an exploratory, investigative, and diagnostic role. The documentary approach developed here aligns less with the notion of illustrating external facts and more with the experimentation with audiovisual forms capable of penetrating and revealing a system of procedures, relations, and interactions—what I refer to as the border mediascape. From this perspective, it is as if the gaze of cinema can adapt itself to different contexts while remaining tied to a worldly conception of representation. The images it produces do not come out of nowhere; they are always generated at a crossroads, through comparison with other devices and techniques, while taking into account the realities on the ground. Although different, the films analyzed all share the goal of restoring visibility to a world that is often reduced to data and controlled through the strategic management of that data. Such visibility thus becomes a precondition for recognition, as well as for the practices and forms of exchange and dialogue that emerge through reciprocity. Without intending to forget the risks of a cinematic spectacularization of the frontier or the forms of complicity between the filmmakers' gaze and the border apparatus, which emerged repeatedly in the pages of the book, cinema wields a geopolitical force that challenges the absolutization of borders and exposes their relativity.

Conceiving a cinematic itinerary at the edge of Europe involves recognizing cinema's potential for inquiry and critique, shedding light on the power dynamics and practices that shape specific contexts. Perhaps precisely for the sake of its hybrid—technological and artistic— character, cinema stands in a liminal position, always investigating and taking part in the regeneration of the relational space. Cinema would in this sense be understood as a form of intermedial inquiry, capable of showing the functioning of other technologies and components that take part in the establishment of their milieus. If *tracking spaces, bodies, and movements* is the primary function of border technologies, then *filming at the border* can render the complexity and dynamism of any environment, showcasing the distinctive features of each body and the reasons for its movement. Through the constraints of framing and the ability to connect different shots through montage, whether in contiguous or dislocated areas, each film enters into a critical dialogue with the techniques that define and delimit sociopolitical life.

Filming at the border sheds light on the processes that determine new borders, establish varied modes of access and circulation, and reproduce discriminations. This approach offers a new vision for investigating the idea of border by exploring its medial thickness, that is, its thickness as a medium. As a mediascape, the border is revealed as an area where control devices are intensified. It is a space of detection, identification, and witnessing, a site of conflict and camouflage, and a stage for rhetoric and spectacle. For some, it is a place of national pride or shame, yet the border is also a place where sensitivity is heightened and, most hopefully, a space for contact, assembly, and creation in continual movement.

FILMOGRAPHY

The book references a vast body of film, literary, and artistic works. This filmography includes only those films or video installations that are analyzed or mentioned in the text and were either shot in European border areas or explicitly related to migration phenomena in the new millennium.

Abdullahi, Ahmed, David Aronowitsch, Sharmarke Binyusuf, and Anna Persson. 2015. *I Am Dublin (Jag är Dublin).*

Ai Weiwei. 2017. *Human Flow.*

Aiello, Michele, and Davide Crudetti, with Ednan Abreu Dos Santos, Rahma Djebali, Jacopo Dragotta, Federico Hu, Ludovica Paesano, Scilla Volpe Simoncelli, and Micaela Zurita Poma. 2019. *Flying Roots.*

Ali Atassi, Mohammad, and Ziad Homsi. 2014. *Our Terrible Country (Baladna alraheeb).*

Al-Kateab, Waad, and Edward Watts. 2019. *For Sama (min ʾajl Samā).*

Alzakout, Amel, and Khaled Abdulwahed. 2020. *Purple Sea (Das Purpurmeer).*

Amiri, Aluk, Hamed Dera, Hevi Dilara, Zakaria Mohamed Ali, and Dagmawi Yimer. 2012. *Welcome to Italy (Benvenuti in Italia).*

Badagliacca, Mario. 2012. *Grooving Lampedusa.*

Biemann, Ursula. 2006–2009. *Sahara Chronicle.*

Brossmann, Jakob. 2015. *Lampedusa in Winter (Lampedusa im Winter).*

Calore, Matteo, and Gustav Hofer. 2014. *Limbo.*

Collizzolli, Stefano. 2019. *Love Has No Borders (L'amour n'a pas de frontière).*

Collizzolli, Stefano, and Matteo Calore. 2011. *Our Best Years (I nostri anni migliori).*

D'Alife, Luigi. 2018. *The Western Border (Il confine occidentale).*

D'Alife, Luigi. 2020. *The Milky Way: Nobody Saves Himself on His Own (The Milky Way: Nessuno si salva da solo).*

Derki, Talal. 2013. *The Return to Homs.*

Dieng Kala, Musa. 2007. *Has God Forsaken Africa? (Dieu a-t-il quitté l'Afrique?).*

Fazili, Hassan. 2019. *Midnight Traveler.*

Fedele, David. 2014. *The Land Between.*

Ferrara, Abel. 2017. *Piazza Vittorio.*

Ferrente, Agostino. 2006. *The Orchestra of Piazza Vittorio (L'orchestra di Piazza Vittorio).*

Forensic Architecture. 2020. *Shipwreck at the Threshold of Europe, Lesvos, Aegean Sea.*

George, Sylvain. 2009. *The Impossible: Pieces of Fury (L'impossible—Pages arrachées).*

George, Sylvain. 2009. *They Will Kill All of Us (Ils nous tuerons tous).*

George, Sylvain. 2010. *May They Rest in Revolt: Figures of War (Qu'ils reposent en révolte—Des figures de guerres 1).*

George, Sylvain. 2011. *Fragments (Les éclats—Ma gueule, ma révolte, mon nom).*

George, Sylvain. 2012. *The Dark Clouds (Les nuées).*

George, Sylvain. 2015. *Nocturne White Hunter (Nocturne Blanc-Chasseur).*

George, Sylvain. 2017. *Paris Is a Movable Feast: A Film in 18 Waves (Paris est une fête: Un film en 18 vagues).*

George, Sylvain. 2022. *Obscure Night: Wild Leaves (Nuit obscure: Feuillets sauvages).*

George, Sylvain. 2023. *Obscure Night: Goodbye Here, Anywhere (Nuit obscure: Au revoir ici, n'importe où).*

George, Sylvain. 2025. *Obscure Night: Ain't I a Child? (Nuit obscure: Ain't I a Child?).*

Heller, Charles, and Lorenzo Pezzani. 2014. *Liquid Traces.*

Heller, Charles, and Lorenzo Pezzani. 2016. *Death by Rescue.*

Heller, Charles, and Lorenzo Pezzani. 2018. *Sea Watch vs the Libyan Coastguard.*

Heller, Charles, and Lorenzo Pezzani. 2018. *The Seizure of the Iuventa.*

Isaacs, Marc. 2003. *Calais: The Last Border.*

Julien, Isaac. 2007. *Western Union: Small Boats.*

KinoMosaik Collective. 2018. *Natives of the New World.*

Köhn, Steffen, and Paola Calvo. 2011. *Tell Me When . . .*

Kourkouta, Maria, and Niki Giannari. 2016. *Spectres Are Haunting Europe (Fantasmata planiountai pano apo tin Europi).*

Kuwornu, Fred Kudjo. 2011. *18 Ius soli.*

Leroyer, Madeleine. 2019. *#387.*

Martino, Paolo. 2012. *Just About My Fingers.*

Martino, Paolo. 2014. *Land of Transit (Terra di transito).*

Melgar, Fernand. 2008. *The Fortress (La forteresse).*

Melgar, Fernand. 2011. *Special Flight (Vol spécial).*

Melgar, Fernand. 2013. *The World Is Like That (Le monde est comme ça).*

Melgar, Fernand. 2014. *The Shelter (L'abri).*

Mohamed Ali, Zakaria. 2013. *To Whom It May Concern.*

Mohammed, Ossama, and Wiam Simav Bedirxan. 2014. *Silvered Water, Syria Self-Portrait (Ma'a al-Fidda).*

Mosse, Richard. 2014–2017. *Incoming.*

Nezam, Alex. 2019. *We Are Not Together.*

Noujaim, Jehane. 2013. *The Square (Al-Maydan).*

Reuschel, Otto. 2017. *Riski.*

Rosi, Gianfranco. 2016. *Fire at Sea (Fuocoammare).*

Rosi, Gianfranco. 2020. *Notturno.*

Rost, Benjamin. 2023. *Harraga: Those Who Burn Their Lives.*

Savona, Stefano. 2011. *Tahrir Liberation Square.*

Segre, Andrea. 2010. *Green Blood (Il sangue verde).*

Segre, Andrea, Matteo Calore, and Stefano Collizzolli. 2023. *Trieste Is Beautiful at Night (Trieste è bella di notte).*

Segre, Andrea, and Stefano Liberti. 2012. *Closed Sea (Mare chiuso).*

Segre, Andrea, Ferruccio Pastore, and Stefano Liberti. 2006. *South of Lampedusa (A sud di Lampedusa).*

Segre, Andrea, Dagmawi Yimer, and Riccardo Biadene. 2008. *Like a Man on Earth (Come un uomo sulla terra).*

Sidibé, Abou Bakar, and Moritz Siebert. 2019. *My New European Life.*

Sidibé, Abou Bakar, Moritz Siebert, and Estephan Wagner. 2016. *Those Who Jump (Les sauteurs).*

Sundberg, Annie, and Ricki Stern. 2007. *The Devil Came on Horseback.*

Van Lancker, Laurent. 2017. *Kalès.*
Waddington, Laura. 2004. *Border.*
Yimer, Dagmawi. 2013. *Va' pensiero.*
Yimer, Dagmawi. 2015. *Asmat—Names in Memory of All the Victims of the Sea.*

NOTES

Introduction

1. Marshall McLuhan, *Understanding Media: The Extensions of Man* (MIT Press, 1994), 358.
2. See Peter Sloterdijk, *Foams: Spheres Volume III: Plural Spherology,* trans. Wieland Hoban (Semiotext(e), 2016), 15.
3. See Ginger Nolan, *The Neocolonialism of the Global Village* (University of Minnesota Press, 2018).
4. Europe and the European Union (EU) do not align perfectly, nor do the Schengen Area and the EU. While administrative, legal, and political distinctions between EU and non-EU countries are certainly significant, border policies produce concrete effects that transcend these territorial and political boundaries. Paradoxically, EU and non–EU borders share a common feature in the ambiguity and violence of their management—for example, the non-EU countries along the Balkan route. For this reason, without underestimating the practical impact of political and territorial differences, this book employs these terms in a flexible manner that seeks to reflect the ambiguity and permeability of EU and non-EU borders within the European continent.
5. See Dario Gentili, "Hic sunt leones. Border/Frontier: The Political Genealogy of a Spatial Disposition," in *Borders of Europe,* ed. Wolfgang Mueller-Funk et al. (Istituto Italiano di Studi Germanici, 2021), 111–21.
6. Sandro Mezzadra and Brett Neilson, *Border as Method, or, the Multiplication of Labor* (Duke University Press, 2013), 15.
7. Mezzadra and Neilson, 14.
8. The opposition between sovereignty and governmentality constitutes the core of Foucault's reflection at least since the 1970s. For a summary of such concepts, that is, on the shift from the political body's claim to impose itself on the national territory to the management of the "men, but men in their relations, their links, their imbrication with those other things which are wealth, resources, means of subsistence, the territory with its specific qualities, climate, irrigation, fertility, etc.," see Michel Foucault, "On Governmentality," *Ideology and Consciousness* 6 (1979): 5–22, quotation on 10. As an introduction to the concept of biopolitics, see Michel Foucault, *The Birth of Biopolitics: Lectures at the Collège de France, 1978–1979,* ed. Michel Senellart, trans. Graham Burchell (Palgrave Macmillan, 2008).
9. Wendy Brown, *Walled States, Waning Sovereignty* (Princeton University Press, 2010), 67.

10. Étienne Balibar, *Politics and the Other Scene,* trans. Christine Jones et al., (Verso Books, 2012), 76.
11. The idea of assemblage is at least partly related to that of *agencement* proposed in Gilles Deleuze and Félix Guattari, *Anti-Oedipus: Capitalism and Schizophrenia,* trans. Robert Hurley et al. (Viking Press, 1977). For its redeployment in the field of media theory, see Francesco Casetti, *The Lumière Galaxy: Seven Keywords for the Cinema to Come* (Columbia University Press, 2015), 67–97. As a reference in border studies, see again Mezzadra and Neilson, *Border as Method,* 195–97.
12. On the environmental character of the media, I refer to Dario Cecchi et al., eds., *Ambienti mediali* (Meltemi, 2018); Andrea Pinotti, "Towards An-Iconology: The Image as Environment." *Screen* 61 (2020): 594–603; Pietro Conte, *Unframing Aesthetics* (Mimesis International, 2020); Giuliana Bruno, *Atmospheres of Projection: Environmentality in Art and Screen Media* (University of Chicago Press, 2022). For an explicit focus on the topic, see *Critical Inquiry* 49 (2023), with papers by Weihong Bao, Jacob Gaboury, Daniel Morgan, Francesco Casetti, D. Cuong O'Neill, Reinhold Martin, Antonio Somaini, Florian Sprenger, and Rahul Mukherjee.
13. Huub Dijstelbloem, *Borders as Infrastructure: The Technopolitics of Border Control* (MIT Press, 2021), 5.
14. Lilie Chouliaraki and Myria Georgiou, *The Digital Border: Migration, Technology, Power* (NYU Press, 2022).
15. On the relationship between cinema, geography, and cartography, I refer to Giuliana Bruno, *Atlas of Emotion: Journeys in Art, Architecture, and Film* (Verso Books, 2002); Tom Conley, *Cartographic Cinema* (University of Minnesota Press, 2007); Chris Lukinbeal and Stefan Zimmerman, eds., *The Geography of Cinema: A Cinematic World* (Franz Steiner Verlag, 2008); Teresa Castro, *La pensée cartographique des images: Cinéma et culture visuelle* (Aléas, 2011); John David Rhodes and Elena Gorfinkel, eds., *Taking Place: Location and the Moving Image* (University of Minnesota Press, 2011); and Giorgio Avezzù, "Film History and 'Cartographic Anxiety,'" in *At the Borders of (Film) History: Temporality, Archaeology, Theories,* ed. Alberto Beltrame et al. (Forum, 2015), 423–30. On cinema's ability to investigate the concept of the border, see Leonardo Quaresima, ed., *Identità, confine: Geografie, modelli, rappresentazioni* (Mimesis, 2021).
16. On the ability of the arts and cinema to intervene in the "partition of the visible," I refer to Jacques Rancière's *The Politics of Aesthetics: The Distribution of the Sensible,* trans. and introduction by Gabriel Rockhill, with an afterword by Slavoj Žižek (Bloomsbury, 2004), *The Intervals of Cinema,* trans. John Howe (Verso Books, 2019), and *The Emancipated Spectator,* trans. Gregory Elliott (Verso Books, 2021).
17. For a reflection that pushes the concept of mediation beyond the idea of technologically assisted communication to view any form of

interaction between humans or nonhumans as a form of mediation, see Richard Grusin, "Radical Mediation," *Critical Inquiry* 42 (2015): 124–48. For a revival and transformation of the semiotic notion of "actant"—proposed by Algirdas Julien Greimas—in critical thought on the Anthropocene, see Bruno Latour, *Facing Gaia: Eight Lectures on the New Climatic Regime,* trans. Catherine Porter (Polity, 2017), 133–34.

18. Suvendrini Perera, "A Pacific Zone? (In)Security, Sovereignty, and Stories of the Pacific Borderscape," in *Borderscapes: Hidden Geographies and Politics at Territory's Edge,* ed. Prem Kumar Rajaram and Carl Grundy-Warr (University of Minnesota Press, 2007), 224.
19. Prem Kumar Rajaram and Carl Grundy-Warr, introduction to *Borderscapes: Hidden Geographies and Politics at Territory's Edge,* ed. Prem Kumar Rajaram and Carl Grundy-Warr (University of Minnesota Press, 2007), ix.
20. Rajaram and Grundy-Warr, xxiv.
21. Arjun Appadurai, *Modernity at Large: Cultural Dimensions of Globalization* (University of Minnesota Press, 1996), 35.
22. Francesco Casetti, "Mediascapes: A Decalogue," *Perspecta* 51 (2018): 24–25.
23. I refer to Friedrich Kittler, *Gramophone, Film, Typewriter,* trans. Geoffrey Winthrop Young and Michael Wutz (Stanford University Press, 1999), for an approach to media that emphasizes their nature as material infrastructures, exploring the concepts of "media technique" *(Medientechnik)* and "cultural technique" *(Kulturtechnik)* and their physical impact on reality. For the development of this perspective in reference to anthropic practices and geopolitical processes, see Bernhard Siegert, *Cultural Techniques: Grids, Filters, Doors, and Other Articulations of the Real* (Fordham University Press, 2015).
24. On media infrastructure as a form of territorial control, see Helga Tawil-Souri, "Cellular Borders: Dis/Connecting Phone Calls in Israel–Palestine," in *Signal Traffic: Critical Studies of Media Infrastructures,* ed. Lisa Parks and Nicole Starosielski (University of Illinois Press, 2015), 157–80.
25. Gilbert Simondon, *On the Mode of Existence of Technical Objects,* trans. Cecile Malaspina and John Rogove (Univocal, 2016), 59.
26. Simondon, 141.
27. The opposition between "stable" and "metastable" systems constitutes one of the theoretical cornerstones developed in Gilbert Simondon, *Individuation in Light of Notions of Form and Information,* vols. 1 and 2, trans. Taylor Adkins (University of Minnesota Press, 2020).
28. On environmental mediation, see John Durham Peters, *The Marvelous Clouds: Towards a Philosophy of Elemental Media* (University of Chicago Press, 2015).
29. On the difference between "strategies" and "tactics," to which we

will return several times in the following pages, I refer to the classic study by Michel de Certeau, *The Practice of Everyday Life*, vol. 1, trans. Steven Rendall (University of California Press, 1988).

30. On the idea of "borderlands resilience" understood as "examination of the situational practices, experiences and narratives of borders, border crossing and belongings from the perspective of adaptation and resistance among different groups and communities," see Dorte Jagetic Andersen and Eeva-Kaisa Prokkola, "Introduction: Embedding Borderlands Resilience," in *Borderlands Resilience: Transition, Adaptation, and Resistance at Borders* (Routledge, 2022), 6.
31. For the development of an intersectional perspective, see Kimberlé Crenshaw, "Demarginalizing the Intersection of Race and Sex: A Black Feminist Critique of Antidiscrimination Doctrine, Feminist Theory and Antiracist Politics," in *Feminist Legal Theories*, ed. Karen Marschke (Routledge, 2013), 23–51; and Avtar Brah and Ann Phoenix, "Ain't I a Woman? Revisiting Intersectionality," *Journal of International Women's Studies* 5, no. 3 (2004): 75–86. I also refer to Donna J. Haraway, "A Cyborg Manifesto: Science, Technology, and Socialist-Feminism in the Late Twentieth Century," in *Simians, Cyborgs, and Women: The Reinvention of Nature* (Routledge, 1991), 149–81; and Rosi Braidotti, "'We' Are in This Together, but We Are Not One and the Same," *Journal of Bioethical Inquiry* 17, no. 4 (2020): 465–69. For a broadening of the epistemological boundaries of intersectionality that takes on contemporary political and ecological challenges and explicitly opens to the idea of alliance between human and nonhuman entities, see Lidia Curti, "Towards a Tentacular Coexistence: Speculative Fiction and Feminist Futures," *de genere: Rivista di studi letterari, postcoloniali e di genere* 3 (2017): 15–23.
32. See Homi Bhabha, *The Location of Culture* (Routledge, 1994).
33. See Hannah Arendt, "We Refugees," in *International Refugee Law*, ed. Hélène Lambert (Routledge, 2016), 3–12. For a theoretical reflection on contemporary forms of migration that develops from the Arendtian hypothesis, see Andrea Cavalletti and Gianluca Solla, eds., *L'avanguardia dei nostri popoli: Per una filosofia della migrazione* (Cronopio, 2020).
34. See W. E. B. Du Bois, *The Souls of Black Folk* (Oxford University Press, 2008).
35. Paul Gilroy, *After Empire: Melancholia or Convivial Culture?* (Routledge, 2004), 41.
36. Achille Mbembe, *Brutalism*, trans. Steven Corcoran (Duke University Press, 2024), xiii.
37. Mbembe, 5.
38. See Whitney Battle-Baptiste and Britt Rusert, eds., *W. E. B. Du Bois's Data Portraits: Visualizing Black America* (Chronicle Books, 2018), and Alexander G. Weheliye, "Diagrammatics as Physiognomy: W. E. B.

Du Bois's Graphic Modernities," *CR: The New Centennial Review* 15, no. 2 (2015): 23–58.

39. On the opposition between the line and colors, see Giorgio Vasari, *Vasari and Technique,* ed. Louisa S. Maclehose and Gerard Baldwin Brown (Dover, 2011), 205. This issue can be therefore found in the opposition between an "optical" conception of vision to a "tactile" or "haptic" (*Taktisch* and *Haptisch*) one, as investigated in Alois Riegl, *Late Roman Art Industry,* trans. Rolf Winkes (G. Bretschneider, 1985), 19–50, or in the treatise on "trait" conducted in Hubert Damisch, *Traité du trait: Tractatus tractus* (Musée du Louvre, 2005). For a theory of the line, considered in its aesthetic, cognitive, and social implications, I refer to Tim Ingold's *The Life of Lines* (Routledge, 2015).
40. McLuhan, *Understanding Media,* 5.
41. For a theoretical revival of the notion of "pointillism" within geographical studies, as well as for an explication of the fact that with the establishment of the "pointillist logic of coordinates, there is no longer this tight relationship between geographic legibility and political authority. Electronic coordinates are explicitly designed to exceed the boundaries of individual states, and maintaining a virtual grid does not require any long-term geographic commitment or sustained control over a contiguous expanse of land," see William Rankin, *After the Map: Cartography, Navigation, and the Transformation of Territory in the Twentieth Century* (University of Chicago Press, 2016), 4.
42. Shahram Khosravi, *"Illegal" Traveller: An Auto-Ethnography of Borders* (Palgrave Macmillan, 2010).
43. Alessandro Leogrande, *La frontiera* (Feltrinelli, 2017), 314. In the same vein, I also refer to the ten-scene musical drama *Haye: The Words, the Night* (*Haye: Le parole, la notte,* 2017), with libretto by Alessandro Leogrande, music by Mauro Montalbetti, and direction by Alina Marazzi.
44. On the "mobile border," see Anne-Laure Amilhat Szary and Frédéric Giraut, eds., *Borderities and Politics of Contemporary Mobile Borders* (Palgrave Macmillan, 2015).
45. Roberto Esposito, *Immunitas: The Protection and Negation of Life,* trans. Zakiya Hanafi (Polity, 2011), 6.
46. On the immunity-based logic underpinning European borders, see Nick Vaughan-Williams, *Europe's Border Crisis: Biopolitical Security and Beyond* (Oxford, 2015), 94–120. Regarding the pandemic scenario, see at least Hank Scotch, ed., "Posts from the Pandemics," *Critical Inquiry* 47 (2021): S1–S142. Expressly on the relations between mediation and immunization, I refer to Francesco Zucconi, "Mediazione e immunizzazione," *Studi culturali* 17 (2020): 221–32, and Matteo Treleani and Francesco Zucconi, eds., "Remediating Distances," *IMG Journal* 3 (2020): 1–499.

47. For a theory of screening as shielding, see Mauro Carbone and Graziano Lingua, *Toward an Anthropology of Screens: Showing and Hiding, Exposing and Protecting* (Palgrave Macmillan, 2023). For a military genealogy of the relationship between screen and shield, see Nicola Perugini and Neve Gordon, *Human Shields: A History of People in the Line of Fire* (University of California Press, 2020), 43–53. For a link between screen media and contemporary border management practices, see Richard Grusin, "La médiation radicale et le pouvoir des écrans," in *Des pouvoirs des écrans*, ed. Mauro Carbone et al. (Editions Mimesis, 2022).
48. For the development of a theory of "protective media," see Francesco Casetti, *Screening Fears: On Protective Media* (Zone Books, 2023).
49. Francesco Zucconi, *Displacing Caravaggio: Art, Media, and Humanitarian Visual Culture*, trans. Zakiya Hanafi (Palgrave Macmillan, 2018).
50. On the idea of developing theoretical and critical thinking through confrontation with specific artistic objects, see Hubert Damisch et al., "A Conversation with Hubert Damisch," *October* 85 (Summer 1998): 3–17. The idea of theoretical object is addressed in Giovanni Careri et al., "L'image et l'affect inséparables: Entretien avec Giovanni Careri," *Images Re-vues: Histoire, anthropologie et théorie de l'art* 20 (2023), https://doi.org/10.4000/imagesrevues.14534. For a rethinking of the idea of theoretical object in relation to cinema, see Jacques Aumont, *À quoi pensent les films* (Séguier Editions, 1996). On film works as forms of thought and critical interrogation of the present time, see Roberto De Gaetano, *Critica del visuale* (Orthotes, 2022).
51. Mieke Bal, *Double Exposures: The Subject of Cultural Analysis* (Routledge, 1996).
52. Iain Chambers, *Location, Borders, and Beyond: Thinking with Postcolonial Art* (Worlding the Word, 2018).
53. Georges Didi-Huberman, *The Eye of History: When Images Take Positions*, trans. Shane B. Lillis (MIT Press, 2018).
54. Reflection on the forms of documentary cinema is constantly expanding. I refer to Erik Barnouw, *Documentary: A History of the Non-Fiction Film* (Oxford University Press, 1993); Michael Renov, *The Subject of Documentary* (University of Minnesota Press, 2004); Stella Bruzzi, *New Documentary* (Routledge, 2006); Ivelise Perniola, *L'era postdocumentaria* (Mimesis, 2014); Marco Bertozzi, *Documentario come arte: Riuso, performance, autobiografia nell'esperienza del cinema contemporaneo* (Marsilio, 2018); and Daniele Dottorini, *La passione del reale: Il documentario o la creazione del mondo* (Mimesis, 2018).
55. In the different chapters, I will reconstruct the debates related to individual films. As general references, capable of providing an overview of the different types of films made on the themes of migration and borders, see Jakub Kazechi et al., eds., *Border Visions: Identity*

and Diaspora in Film (Scarecrow Press, 2013); Giorgio Bertellini, "Film, National Cinema, and Migration," *The Encyclopedia of Global Human Migration* 3 (2013): 1504–9; Nilgun Bayraktar, *Mobility and Migration in Film and Moving Image Art: Cinema Beyond Europe* (Routledge, 2015); Monica Hannah and Rebecca A. Sheehan, eds., *Border Cinema: Reimagining Identity Through Aesthetics* (Rutgers University Press, 2019); Massimiliano Coviello and Giacomo Tagliani, "Migrant Images and Imageries in Contemporary Italian Cinema," *L'avventura: International Journal of Italian Film and Media Landscapes* 5 (2019): 227–40; Raita Merivirta et al., eds., *Frontiers of Screen History: Imagining European Borders in Cinema, 1945–2010* (Intellect, 2013); Juliet Steyn and Nadja Stamselberg, eds., *Breaching Borders: Art, Migrants and the Metaphor of Waste* (I.B. Tauris, 2014); Isolina Ballesteros, *Immigration Cinema in the New Europe* (Intellect, 2015); Adrian Bremenkamp et al., eds., *Geografie della migrazione nel cinema Italiano: Luoghi e immaginari del transito* (Campisano, 2022); and Deniz Bayrakdar and Robert Burgoyne, eds., *Refugees and Migrants in Contemporary Film, Art, and Media* (Amsterdam University Press, 2022).

56. Gayatri Chakravorty Spivak, "Can the Subaltern Speak?," in *Marxism and the Interpretation of Culture,* ed. Cary Nelson and Lawrence Grossberg (University of Illinois Press, 1988), 271–313.
57. For research that separates into two different sections—but in fact holds together within the volume—the study of films in which the perspective of the migrant is taken and those in which the migration phenomenon is subject to an external perspective, see Nicole Beth Wallenbrock and Frank Jacob, eds., *Migrants' Perspectives, Migrants in Perspective: World Cinema* (Edinburgh University Press, 2021).
58. On this point, see Christian Rossipal, "Poetics of Refraction: Mediterranean Migration and New Documentary Forms," *Film Quarterly* 74, no. 3 (2021): 35–45.
59. Just to mention a few titles, the season of the Arab Spring is at the center of works such as *Tahrir Liberation Square* (2011) by Stefano Savona and *The Square* (*Al-Maydan,* 2013) by Jehane Noujaim, while the aftermath of the war in Afghanistan can be found in *Midnight Traveler* (2019) by Hassan Fazili. The violence of the Syrian War is investigated in works such as *The Return to Homs* (2013) by Talal Derki, *Silvered Water, Syria Self-Portrait* (*Ma'a al-Fidda,* 2014) by Ossama Mohammed and Wiam Simav Bedirxan, *Our Terrible Country* (*Baladna alraheeb,* 2014) by Mohammad Ali Atassi and Ziad Homsi, and *For Sama* (*min ʾajl Samā,* 2019) by Waad Al-Kateab and Edward Watts. On the conflicts that have ravaged different countries in central Africa, I mention *The Devil Came on Horseback* (2007) by Annie Sundberg and Ricki Stern, and *Has God Forsaken Africa?* (*Dieu a-t-il quitté l'Afrique?,* 2007) by Musa Dieng Kala. On crossing the Sahara Desert as a geographical and political boundary, I mention

South of Lampedusa (*A sud di Lampedusa,* 2006) by Andrea Segre, in collaboration with Ferruccio Pastore and Stefano Liberti, and *Sahara Chronicle* (2006–9) by Ursula Biemann. Regarding the Eastern Mediterranean context, I briefly mention filmmakers who have explored the region's long history of conflict, dispossession, and destruction, including Avi Mograbi, Mai Masri, Mohammad Bakri, and Eyal Sivan.

60. For a transnational approach to the history of cinema that is aimed at investigating the forms of persistence and transformations of the colonial imprint through the decades, see Lindiwe Dovey, *African Film and Literature: Adapting Violence to the Screen* (Columbia University Press, 2009); Hamid Naficy, *An Accented Cinema: Exilic and Diasporic Filmmaking* (Princeton University Press, 2001); Leonardo De Franceschi, *Lo schermo e lo spettro: Sguardi postcoloniali su Africa e afrodiscendenti* (Mimesis, 2017); Áine O'Healy, *Migrant Anxieties: Italian Cinema in a Transnational Frame* (Indiana University Press, 2019); and Luca Caminati, et al., eds., "Cinema Italiano postcoloniale," *Cinema e storia: Rivista annuale di studi interdisciplinari* 13 (2024): 1–298.

1. Hot and Cold Borders

1. On the shift from an eminently humanitarian conception of borders to a securitarian one, see Didier Fassin, "Signes des temps," in *La raison humanitaire: Une histoire morale du présent* (Éditions de l'École des hautes études en sciences sociales, Gallimard and Seuil, 2018), 411–27. On the transition between Mare Nostrum and Triton, see Martina Tazzioli, "Border Displacements: Challenging the Politics of Rescue Between Mare Nostrum and Triton." *Migration Studies* 4, no. 1 (2016): 1–19. On the history of Frontex, see Nina Perkowski, *Humanitarianism, Human Rights, and Security: The Case of Frontex* (Routledge, 2021).
2. See Pierluigi Musarò, "Mare Nostrum: The Visual Politics of a Military-Humanitarian Operation in the Mediterranean Sea," *Media, Culture & Society* 39 (2017): 11–28.
3. For a polyphony of voices and approaches on the topic of recognition I refer to the various essays in *Recognition and Ambivalence,* ed. Heikki Ikäheimo et al. (Columbia University Press, 2021).
4. For an ethical and political reflection on the different forms of intersubjective recognition in the contemporary scenario, see Louise Amoore, *Cloud Ethics: Algorithms and the Attributes of Ourselves and Others* (Duke University Press, 2020).
5. See Carmelo Marabello, "Quotidiano," in *Lessico del cinema Italiano: Forme di rappresentazione e forme di vita,* vol. 3, ed. Roberto De Gaetano (Mimesis, 2016), 87–88.
6. References to the critical debate on *Fire at Sea* are given in the notes throughout this article. For a survey of criticism of *Fire at Sea,* see

Elvira Pulitano, *Mediterranean ARTivism: Art, Activism, and Migration in Europe* (Palgrave Macmillan, 2020), 136–47.

7. See Gemma Sou, *"Fire at Sea (Fuocoammare),"* *Nationalities Papers* 46 (2018): 335–36; and Giuliano Migliori, "Revisualizing the Human Body in Crialese and Rosi's Cinematic Narratives," *L'avventura: International Journal of Italian Film and Media Landscapes* 1 (2021): 113–28.
8. The analysis of *Fire at Sea* has mostly overlooked the importance of the control technologies shown in the film, although the director himself has stressed this aspect on several occasions. See Yonca Talu, "Interview: Gianfranco Rosi," *Film Comment*, October 24, 2016, https://www.filmcomment.com/blog/interview-gianfranco-rosi-fire-at-sea.
9. For a critical reflection on the impact of control technologies present on the island of Lampedusa, see Lorenzo Alunni, *Le cicatrici di Ulisse: Corpi e frontiere nel Mediterraneo* (Meltemi, 2024), 181–211. On the capacity of Fire at Sea to produce "a sensory perception of Lampedusa as a relational space," see Sudeep Dasgupta, "*Fuocoammare* and the Aesthetic Rendition of the Relational Experience of Migration," in *Handbook of Art and Global Migration: Theories, Practices, and Challenges*, ed. Burcu Dogramaci and Birgit Mersman (De Gruyter, 2019), 102–16. On this point, see also Lidia De Michelis, "Of Islands and Bears: The Aesthetics and Politics of Gianfranco Rosi's *Fuocoammare*," in *Migration and the Contemporary Mediterranean: Shifting Cultures in Twenty-First-Century Italy and Beyond*, ed. Claudia Gualtieri (De Gruyter, 2018), 320–21. Also on this point, with reference to Rosi's previous films, from *Below Sea Level* (2008) to *Sacro GRA* (2013), see Marco Bertozzi, *Documentario come arte: Riuso, performance, autobiografia nell'esperienza del cinema contemporaneo* (Marsilio, 2018), 80–81.
10. Marshall McLuhan, *Understanding Media: The Extensions of Man* (MIT Press, 1994), 22–23.
11. For a rethinking of the opposition proposed by McLuhan, see Francesco Casetti and Antonio Somaini, eds., *La haute et la basse définition des images: Photographie, cinéma, art contemporain, culture visuelle* (Editions Mimesis, 2021); and Nicole Starosielski, *Media Hot & Cold* (Duke University Press, 2022).
12. Toward an expanded understanding of mediation, see Richard Grusin, "Radical Mediation," *Critical Inquiry* 42 (2015): 124–48. On the attention brought by Rosi to the time that migrants spend waiting and how they interact and contact with the rescue agents, see Emma Wilson, "From Lampedusa to the California Desert: Gianfranco Rosi's Scenes of Living and Dying," *Film Quarterly* 71, no. 3 (March 2018): 13–14, https://doi.org/10.1525/fq.2018.71.3.10.
13. For a reflection on the devices that make it possible to "see" in lighting and atmospheric conditions that are incompatible with the

human eye, see Ruggero Eugeni, *Capitale algoritmico: Cinque dispositivi postmediali (più uno)* (Scholè, 2021), 83–125.

14. On biopolitical governance technologies of borders and transit areas, see Lauren B. Wilcox, *Bodies of Violence: Theorizing Embodied Subjects in International Relations* (Oxford University Press, 2015). On the idea of the "border-bodies," see Achille Mbembe, *Brutalism*, trans. Steven Corcoran (Duke University Press, 2024), 78–90.
15. Expressly on the problem of recognition in biomedical technologies, see Amoore, *Cloud Ethics*, 160–64.
16. See Eithne Luibhéid, *Pregnant on Arrival: Making the Illegal Immigrant* (University of Minnesota Press, 2013); Camille Schmoll, *Les damnées de la mer: Femmes et frontières en Méditerranée* (La Découverte, 2020); and Vanessa Grotti et al., "Temporalities of Emergency: Migrant Pregnancy and Healthcare Networks in Southern European Borderlands," *Social Science & Medicine* 222 (2019): 11–19.
17. For a reconsideration of the Foucauldian notion of "biopolitics" in an affirmative key, see Roberto Esposito, "Community, Immunity, Biopolitics," *Angelaki* 18, no. 3 (2013): 83–90. For an explicit reference to pregnancy as a condition in which a rotation of the immune paradigm takes place—"from a defense barrier against the outside to a process of differential transformation of the very subjects it identifies"—see Roberto Esposito, *Living Thought: The Origins and Actuality of Italian Philosophy*, trans. Zakiya Hanafi (Stanford University Press, 2012), 261–62.
18. For a reflection on the cinematic memory summoned by Rosi's film that develops in a different direction, see Daniel Winkler, "Intermediale Strategien in Jakob Brossmanns *Lampedusa im Winter* (2015) und Gianfranco Rosi's *Fuocoammare* (2016)," *Romanische Forschungen* 132 (2020): 193–219.
19. Stefania Parigi, *Neorealismo: Il nuovo cinema del dopoguerra* (Marsilio, 2014), 41. Translation is mine. On the relationship between De Robertis and the fascist regime, as well as on its influence on postwar cinema, see Francesco Pitassio, *Neorealist Film Culture, 1945–1954: Rome, Open Cinema* (Amsterdam University Press, 2019), 57–58.
20. On the representation of the maritime landscape in De Robertis's cinema, I refer to Francesco Zucconi, "Geografia," in *Lessico del cinema Italiano: Forme di rappresentazione e forme di vita*, vol. 1, ed. Roberto De Gaetano (Mimesis, 2014), 454–56.
21. On the idea that Rosi's film limits itself to "encourage compassion and pity in the viewer, through a spectacle of suffering that locates the migrants—and to some extent also the locals—at the usual space of invisibility they commonly inhabit in all mainstream representations, failing to encourage a more sophisticated understanding of the issue of immigration to Lampedusa," see Federica Mazzara, *Reframing Migration: Lampedusa, Border Spectacle, and the Aesthetics of*

Subversion (Peter Lang, 2019), 49–50. On the fact that "We never hear any of the migrants directly, or their personal story," see Sandra Ponzanesi, "Of Shipwrecks and Weddings: Borders and Mobilities in Europe," *Transnational Cinemas* 7, no. 2 (2016): 163.

22. The problematic relationship between the film and the military machine is highlighted in a note from the Askavusa Collective, which is active on the island of Lampedusa and particularly committed to issues of migration and citizenship: "*Fuocoammare*: Considerazioni del Collettivo Askavusa," *Askavusa*, February 24, 2016, https://askavusa.wordpress.com/2016/02/24/1428/.
23. For a development of this idea, see Nicholas De Genova, "Migrant 'Illegality' and Deportability in Everyday Life," *Annual Review of Anthropology* 31 (2002): 419–47; and Paolo Cuttitta, *Lo spettacolo del confine: Lampedusa tra produzione e messa in scena della frontiera* (Mimesis, 2012).
24. On the political implications of the radio and telephone messages shown in the film, see Emma Wilson, "Telephone Calls in Gianfranco Rosi's *Fire at Sea* (*Fuocoammare*, 2016)," *Alphaville: Journal of Film and Screen Media* 18 (2019): 12–23. On the idea that "*Fire at Sea* is full of visual metaphors for 'seeing,'" see Adam Vaughan, "Documenting Difference: Migration and Identity in European Documentaries," in *European Cinema in the Twenty-First Century: Discourses, Directions, and Genres*, ed. Ingrid Lewis and Laura Canning (Palgrave Macmillan, 2020), 27.
25. Jean Epstein, "Le cinématographe vu de l'Etna," in *Jean Epstein: Critical Essays and New Translations*, ed. Sarah Keller and Jason N. Paul (Amsterdam University Press), 287–310.
26. Jean Epstein, "L'ONU confie onze films à onze nations différentes," radio interview, 1950, cited in James Schneider, "Cinema Seen from the Seas: Epstein and the Oceanic," *Jean Epstein: Critical Essays and New Translations*, 199.
27. Schneider, 199.
28. On the importance of the sea within the film as a "contradictory element," see Kaisa Hiltunen, "Recent Documentary Films About Migration: In Search of Common Humanity," *Studies in Documentary Film* 13, no. 2 (2019): 141–55.
29. John Durham Peters, *The Marvelous Clouds: Towards a Philosophy of Elemental Media* (University of Chicago Press, 2015), 115.
30. Gilbert Simondon, *On the Mode of Existence of Technical Objects*, trans. Cecile Malaspina and John Rogove (Univocal, 2016), 178.
31. I refer to the AMM's website, which collects and disseminates self-reports and written and oral accounts of migration. https://www.archiviomemoriemigranti.net.
32. Mieke Bal, *Double Exposures: The Subject of Cultural Analysis* (Routledge, 1996), 9.

33. For a psychoanalytic reflection on the importance of the close-up in Rosi's film, see Giuseppina Antinucci, "The Uncanny Encounter or the Encounter with the Uncanny Other: The Work of Identity and Its Transformations in *Fuocoammare*: From Being Lost at Sea to Coming into Being," *International Journal of Psychoanalysis* 101, no. 2, (2020): 388–401.
34. Martine Kaluszynski, "Alphonse Bertillon et l'anthropométrie," in *Maintien de l'ordre et polices en France et en Europe au XIXe siècle,* ed. Alaine Faure and Philippe Vigier (Ed. Creaphis, 1987), 269–85.
35. Paul Knepper and Per Jørgen Ystehede, eds., *The Cesare Lombroso Handbook* (Routledge, 2014).
36. Kelly A. Gates, *Our Biometric Future: Facial Recognition Technology and the Culture of Surveillance* (New York University Press, 2011).
37. Emmanuel Levinas, *Totality and Infinity: An Essay on Exteriority,* trans. Alphonso Lingis (Martinus Nijhoff Publishers and Duquesne University Press, 1979), 74–75.
38. See Luc Boltanski, *Distant Suffering: Morality, Media and Politics,* trans. Graham Burchell (Cambridge University Press, 1999).
39. On these terms, I refer to the classic study by Pierre Bourdieu, *Distinction: A Social Critique of the Judgement of Taste,* trans. Richard Nice (Harvard University Press, 1996), 169–225.
40. Jean-Luc Nancy, *Portrait,* trans. Sarah Clift and Simon Sparks (Fordham University Press, 2018), 45.
41. On the representation of the face and the look-to-the-camera in film history and its effects in the viewers, see Vittorio Gallese and Michele Guerra, *The Empathic Screen: Cinema and Neuroscience,* trans. Frances Anderson (Oxford University Press, 2020), 145–79. With reference to its political function in Rosi's film, see Alessia Cervini, "Cinefilia e militanza: *Fuocoammare* di Gianfranco Rosi," *il lavoro culturale,* February 25, 2016, https://www.lavoroculturale.org/fuocoammare-gianfranco-rosi/alessia-cervini.
42. Serge Daney, *Postcards from the Cinema,* trans. Paul Grant (Berg, 2007), 35.

2. Operational Frontiers

1. For a reflection on the Cutro massacre starting from changes in the management of Mediterranean borders over the past few years, see Lorenzo Alunni and Didier Fassin, "EU's Criminal Policy Is Playing Out in the Mediterranean Amidst General Indifference," *Le Monde,* March 10, 2023, https://www.lemonde.fr/en/opinion/article/2023/03/10/eu-s-criminal-policy-is-playing-out-in-the-mediterranean-amidst-general-indifference601881923.html.
2. For the prime minister's statements after the Cutro massacre, see "Meloni: 'Andremo a cercare gli scafisti lungo tutto il globo terracqueo': E il video diventa virale," *La Repubblica,* March 10, 2023, https://

video.repubblica.it/dossier/governo-meloni-video-interviste-dirette/meloni-andremo-a-cercare-gli-scafisti-lungo-tutto-il-globo-terracqueo-e-il-video-diventa-virale/439933/440897. Translation is mine.

3. The NGO posted the video with the phone recording on its social channels. For a reconstruction of the communication, see Giuseppe Legato, "'Grazie delle informazioni, ciao': La risposta all'Sos di Sea Watch imbarazza la Guardia Costiera. La replica: 'Non c'erano i mezzi,'" *La Stampa,* March 14, 2003, https://www.lastampa.it/cronaca/2023/03/14/news/migranti_guardia_costiera_polemica_sea_watch-12692613/.
4. For a detailed presentation of the center's goals and activities, see https://forensic-architecture.org/about/agency.
5. Allan Sekula, "Photography and the Limits of National Identity," *Culture Front* 2, no. 3 (1993): 54–55. For a resumption of this idea, see Thomas Keenan, "Counter-forensics and Photography," *Grey Room* 55 (2014): 58–77.
6. Eyal Weizman, *Forensic Architecture: Violence at the Threshold of Detectability* (Zone Books, 2017), 309.
7. Yve-Alain Bois et al., "On Forensic Architecture: A Conversation with Eyal Weizman," *October* 156 (2016): 124.
8. Matthew Fuller and Eyal Weizman, *Investigative Aesthetics: Conflicts and Commons in the Politics of Truth* (Verso Books, 2021), 4.
9. For historical, theoretical, and critical reflection on Farocki's work, see the various essays in Thomas Elsaesser, ed., *Harun Farocki: Working on the Sight-Lines* (Amsterdam University Press, 2004).
10. Harun Farocki, *War Always Finds a Way,* in *HF/RG,* ed. Chantal Pontbriand (Jeu de Paume/Blackjack Editions, 2009), 107.
11. See Trevor Paglen, "Operational Images," *e-flux* 59 (2014), http://e-flux.com/journal/59/61130/operational-images/; Hito Steyerl, *Duty Free Art* (Verso Books, 2017); and T. J. Demos, *Beyond the World's End: Arts of Living at the Crossing* (Duke University Press, 2020). For a thought that brings film theory and the question of machine vision together, see Antonio Somaini, "Film Theory and Machine Vision," in *The Oxford Handbook of Film Theory,* ed. Kyle Stevens (Oxford University Press, 2022).
12. See Weizman, *Forensic Architecture,* 97 and, for an explicit reference to Farocki, note 68.
13. For a reflection on operational images as the intertwining point between the reflection on "cultural techniques" and that on "operative ontologies," with reference to Bernhard Siegert, Michel Serres, Brian Massumi, Karen Barad, and others, see Jussi Parikka, *Operational Images: From the Visual to the Invisual* (Minnesota University Press, 2023).
14. On the relationship between image and environment, in a line of

thought that connects artists such as Dziga Vertov, Harun Farocki, and Michael Snow, as well as a juxtaposition between the idea of *operative Bilder* and that of "expanded cinema," see David Tomas, ed., *Vertov, Snow, Farocki: Machine Vision and the Posthuman* (Bloomsbury, 2013).

15. As a foundational study for thinking about the relationship between image and war, as well as the idea of a logistics of perception, I refer to Paul Virilio, *War and Cinema: The Logistics of Perception* (Verso Books, 1989). The relationship between "operational aesthetics" and logistics is explicitly addressed in Parikka, *Operational Images,* 162–72.
16. See Volker Pantenburg, "Working Image: Harun Farocki and the Operational Image," in *Image Operations: Visual Media and Political Conflict,* ed. Jens Eder and Charlotte Klonk (Manchester University Press, 2017); Maurizio Guerri, "Le immagini operative e le guerre contemporanee in Harun Farocki," in *Harun Farocki: Pensare con gli occhi,* ed. Luisella Farinotti et al. (Mimesis, 2017), 321–35; and Samuel Antichi, *Shooting Back. Il documentario e le guerre del nuovo millennio* (Meltemi, 2023), 127–73.
17. Gilbert Simondon, *On the Mode of Existence of Technical Objects,* trans. Cecile Malaspina and John Rogove (Univocal, 2016), 57.
18. Gilbert Simondon, *Individuation in Light of Notions of Form and Information,* vol. 2, trans. Taylor Adkins (University of Minnesota Press, 2020), 685.
19. Although they do not refer to Farocki or to the operational function of images and media, I see important possibilities for dialogue with the reflections developed in Sandro Mezzadra and Brett Neilson, *The Politics of Operations: Excavating Contemporary Capitalism* (Duke University Press, 2019).
20. Farocki, *War Always Finds a Way,* 103.
21. Farocki, 103.
22. I use this term referring to the relationships between technological performance and perceptual and cognitive processes, as investigated in Shane Denson, *Discorrelated Images* (Duke University Press, 2020).
23. I refer to Paul Virilio, *Desert Screen: War at the Speed of Light,* trans. Michael Degener (Continuum, 2002).
24. For a reflection on Farocki's cinema that focuses on the question of the archive and investigates its aesthetic, ethical, and political implications, see Christa Blümlinger, "Harun Farocki: Critical Strategies," in Elsaesser, *Harun Farocki,* 320–21.
25. On the aesthetic, cognitive, and critical orientations of montage in Farocki, in comparison with twentieth-century montage aesthetics, see Georges Didi-Huberman, *Remontages du temps subi: L'œil de l'histoire, 2* (Minuit, 2010), 71–195; and Nicole Brenez, "Harun Farocki and the Romantic Genesis of the Principle of Visual Critique," in

Harun Farocki: Against What? Against Whom?, ed. Antje Ehmann and Kodwo Eshun (Koenig Books), 128–42.

26. See https://forensic-architecture.org/category/forensic-oceanography. The reconstruction of the origin of these projects and further developments is beyond the scope of this book. I merely refer here to the subsequent founding of the Border Forensics research center by Heller and Pezzani, now directed by Charles Heller. See https://www.borderforensics.org/.
27. Fuller and Weizman, *Investigative Aesthetics*, 69.
28. Fuller and Weizman, 69.
29. For an analysis of *Liquid Traces* see Demos, *Beyond the World's End*, 90–91; and Massimiliano Coviello, "Interrogare il Mediterraneo: Fenomeni migratori, tracce liquide, e documenti probatori," *Carte Semiotiche. Rivista Internazionale di Semiotica e Teoria dell'Immagine*, no. 4 (2016): 42–51.
30. On how to reconstruct the ship's trajectory to the point of drift using oceanographic expertise, see Charles Heller and Lorenzo Pezzani, "Forensic Oceanography: The Deadly Drift of a Migrant's Boat in the Central Mediterranean," in *Forensis: The Architecture of Public Truth* (Sternberg Press, 2014), 639–48.
31. In addition to the references provided in the previous chapters on elemental media, for a "media archaeology of the sea" that explicitly refers to the work of FA and FO, see Bernhard Siegert, *Final Frontiers: Eine Medienarchäologie des Meeres* (Brill, 2024), xvii–xviii. On the relationship between media and meteorology, see Mark B. N. Hansen and William John Thomas Mitchell, introduction to *Critical Terms for Media Studies*, ed. William John Thomas Mitchell and Mark B. N. Hansen (University of Chicago Press, 2010). Still on the rapport between media and weather, see Yuriko Furuhata, *Climatic Media: Transpacific Experiments in Atmospheric Control* (Duke University Press, 2022).
32. Fernand Braudel, *La Mediterranée: L'espace et l'histoire* (Flammarion, 1985), 58. Translation is mine. For a research perspective that highlights historical processes and power relations—emphasizing human agency and cultural encounters in the Mediterranean, I refer to David Abulafia, *The Great Sea: A Human History of the Mediterranean* (Oxford University Press, 2011).
33. I refer here to Derrida's classic study *Of Grammatology*, trans. Gayatri Chakravorty Spivak (Johns Hopkins University Press, 1997). See also *Cinders*, with an introduction by Cary Wolfe, trans. Ned Lukacher (Minnesota University Press, 2014).
34. See Bernard Stiegler, *Technics and Time, 1: The Fault of Epimetheus*, trans. Richard Beardsworth (Stanford University Press, 1998), and the two subsequent volumes of this series.
35. Regarding maps as both forms of representation and instruments

of power, I refer to Louis Marin's classic work *On Representation*, trans. Catherine Porter (Stanford University Press, 2001), 202–18. On the idea that "The map is the territory inasmuch as, for instance, map-making is a cultural technique that, in the service of the state, produced the territory as a political reality," see Bernhard Siegert, "The Map *Is* the Territory," *Radical Philosophy* 5 (2011): 13–16.

36. Achille Mbembe, *Necropolitics*, trans. Steven Corcoran (Duke University Press, 2019).
37. See https://forensic-architecture.org/investigation/shipwreck-at-the-threshold-of-europe/. On this project, see Christina Varvia (images by Amel Alzakout), "Image-Sections: The Evidentiary Capacity of Images to Sample the Lifeworld and Have an Operative Life," *Nordic Journal of Aesthetics* 30, nos. 61–62 (2021): 206–29.
38. Anja Sunhyun Michaelsen, "'Locked out in nature': Films on the European Asylum System, Latent Violence, and Ghosts," in *Weathering: Ecologies of Exposure*, ed. Christoph F. E. Holzhey and Arnd Wedemeyer (ICI Berlin Press, 2020); Miren Gutiérrez, "Making Dispersed Data a Visual Event," *Frontiers in Communication* 8 (2023), https://doi.org/10.3389/fcomm.2023.1115270; and Nicolas Appelt, "La réappropriation du récit du conflit dans la distance: Documentaires syriens tournés en exil," *Hommes & Migrations* 1335, no. 4 (2021): 71–79.
39. For a reading of the film that reflects on the processes of rationalization of borders and the idea of human trafficking, see Jon Hackett, "Trafficking on Film: A Critical Survey," in *Modern Slavery and Human Trafficking: The Victim Journey*, ed. Carole Murphy and Runa Lazzarino (Bristol University Press, 2022).
40. Camille Schmoll, *Les damnées de la mer: Femmes et frontières en Méditerranée* (La Découverte, 2020), 71. Translation is mine.
41. On this point see Mariana Duarte, "A Camera in the Water: Reframing the Migrant Image in Documentary Film," *Screen* 65 (2024): 212–32.
42. Amber Wilkinson, *Purple Sea*, "Eye for Film," April 12, 2021, https://www.eyeforfilm.co.uk/review/purple-sea-2020-film-review-by-amber-wilkinson.
43. On the experimental character of this film, see Ohad Landesman, "Here, There, and Everywhere: *Leviathan* and the Digital Future of Observational Ethnography," *Visual Anthropology Review* 31, no. 1 (2015): 12–19; Lisa Stevenson and Eduardo Kohn, "*Leviathan*: An Ethnographic Dream," *Visual Anthropology Review* 31, no. 1 (2015): 49–53; Francesco Zucconi, "Action camera: L'occhio dell'Antropocene?," *Fata Morgana* 28 (2016): 151–57.
44. For a dialogue on the forms of experimental documentary, bringing together the pioneering research of Harvard's Sensory Ethnography Lab and that of a film like *Purple Sea*, see Cynthia Browne et al.,

"Collaborations Across Cinematic Objects: A Conversation Between Pong and Sensory Ethnography Lab, Mediated by the Graduate Research Training Group 'Documentary Practices: Excess and Privation,'" *Visual Anthropology Review* 38, no. 2 (2022): 298–319.

45. For an analysis of *Purple Sea* as a film that "is not a typical first-person documentary, however. While the film offers a meditation on a singular journey and experience, Alzakout's camera doesn't invite the viewer to 'see through her eyes,'" see Christian Rossipal, "Poetics of Refraction: Mediterranean Migration and New Documentary Forms," *Film Quarterly* 74, no. 3 (2021): 41.
46. On the idea of water as an interface, in a research perspective inspired by the media thinking of Vilém Flusser, see Melodie Jue, *Wild Blue Media: Thinking Through Seawater* (Duke University Press, 2022), 34–70.
47. For a thorough analysis of *Asmat* within a reflection on the politics of mourning, see Daniele Salerno, "Stragi del mare e politiche del lutto sul confine mediterraneo," in *Il colore della nazione*, ed. Gaia Giuliani (Mondadori, 2015), 123–39. For an account of the film, at the conclusion of a book on racism and the processes of racialization in twentieth-century and contemporary Italy, see Gaia Giuliani, *Race, Nation, and Gender in Modern Italy: Intersectional Representations in Visual Culture* (Palgrave Macmillan, 2019), 240–52; and Sandra Ponzanesi, "Connecting Shores: Libya's Colonial Ghost and Europe's Migrant Crisis in Colonial and Postcolonial Cinematic Representations," in *Border Lampedusa: Subjectivity, Visibility and Memory in Stories of Sea and Land*, ed. Gabriele Proglio and Laura Odasso (Palgrave Macmillan, 2018), 123–25.
48. I refer to the film presentation on the Archivio Memorie Migranti website: https://www.archiviomemoriemigranti.net/films/co-productions/asmat-names/?lang=en.
49. The reference here is to the idea of the "black Mediterranean," developed in the field of postcolonial studies to challenge traditional narratives of the Mediterranean as a "white" space, highlighting the historical and contemporary presence of black and Afro-descendant communities. See Gabriele Proglio et al., eds., *The Black Mediterranean: Bodies, Borders, and Citizenship* (Springer, 2021). This approach is closely related to Paul Gilroy's proposal to reconstruct a "history of the black Atlantic since then, continually crisscrossed by the movements of black people—not only as commodities but engaged in various struggles towards emancipation, autonomy, and citizenship—provides a means to reexamine the problems of nationality, location, identity, and historical memory." See Paul Gilroy, *The Black Atlantic: Modernity and Double Consciousness* (Harvard University Press, 1993), 16.

50. On this point, through an explicit comparison with Yimer's film, see Iain Chambers, *Postcolonial Interruptions, Unauthorised Modernities* (Rowman & Littlefield, 2017), 126.
51. Charles Heller, "Per una costituente migrante," *il lavoro culturale,* February 7, 2017, https://www.lavoroculturale.org/costituente-migrante-le-frontiere-marittime-delleuropa/charles-heller/2017. Translation is mine.

3. An Archaeology of the Fortress

1. Although not part of the EU, Switzerland is a member of the Schengen Area and supports the activities of the European Border and Coast Guard Agency—Frontex. For an overview of the Swiss context, beyond what is shown in the film, see the Asylum Information Database Report: https://asylumineurope.org/wp-content/uploads/2022/04/AIDA-CH_2021update.pdf.
2. For a critical reflection that brings together governmental protocols and visual forms, see Judith Butler, *Frames of War: When Is Life Grievable?* (Verso Books, 2010), 63–100.
3. I refer, for example, to Pauline Milani, "Migration sur grand écran," in *Sociétés de migrations en débat: Québec–Canada–Suisse: Approches comparées,* ed. Claude Hauser et al. (Pulaval, 2013), 114; Marthe Porret, "Un goût sucré d'asile *(La forteresse),*" *Décadrages* 13 (2008): 28–36; and Jan Kühnemund, "Undocumented Migration in European Borderlands: Relocating the Crisis in Contemporary Documentaries," in *Contemporary European Cinema,* ed. Betty Kaklamanidou and Ana Corbalán (Routledge, 2018), 80–92.
4. For an introduction to the multiple backgrounds of media archaeology, see Jussi Parikka, *What Is Media Archaeology?* (Polity, 2011).
5. Paul Virilio, *Bunker Archeology,* trans. George Collins (Princeton Architectural Press, 2008), 40.
6. Virilio, 30.
7. Virilio, 27.
8. Virilio, 29.
9. Michel Foucault, *Discipline and Punish: The Birth of the Prison,* trans. Alan Sheridan (Vintage Books, 1995), 170–71.
10. Foucault, 172.
11. Gilles Deleuze, *Negotiations 1972–1990,* trans. Martin Joughin (Columbia University Press, 1995), 180.
12. For a discussion of these two concepts with reference to the context of the new millennium, I refer to Alexander R. Galloway, *Protocol: How Control Exists After Decentralization* (MIT Press, 2006).
13. For a synthetic framework on hotspots as "reception centers situated at main points of entry to the territory of the European Union" in geographical areas that are "sufficiently remote to operate at a distance from the gaze of human rights organizations, yet [remain-

ing] inside the perimeter of the Union so as to avoid gross violations of international law," see Didier Fassin, "Hot Spots: What They Mean," *Fieldsights*, June 28, 2016, https://culanth.org/fieldsights/hot-spots-what-they-mean.

14. I refer again to the reconceptualization of McLuhan's thought proposed in chapter 1 of this book.
15. Anja Sunhyun Michaelsen, "'Locked out in nature': Films on the European Asylum System, Latent Violence, and Ghosts," in *Weathering: Ecologies of Exposure*, ed. Christoph F. E. Holzhey and Arnd Wedemeyer (ICI Berlin Press, 2020), 213.
16. On the infrastructure that connects local facilities together, creating a large-scale network, see Huub Dijstelbloem, *Borders as Infrastructure: The Technopolitics of Border Control* (MIT Press, 2021), 25–56.
17. Beyond the film, on the border's ability to function as a "social limit junction," see Thomas Nail, *Theory of the Border* (Oxford University Press, 2016), 21–43.
18. Carl Schmitt, *The "Nomos" of the Earth in the International Law of the "Jus Publicum Europaeum,"* trans. Gary L. Ulmen (Telos Press, 2006), especially 67–80.
19. See Sandro Mezzadra and Brett Neilson, *Border as Method, or, the Multiplication of Labor* (Duke University Press, 2013), 76.
20. I borrow the notion of "border mediascaping" from that of "borderscaping," proposed to reflect on bordering processes and practices in the European context. See Chiara Brambilla et al., eds., *Borderscaping: Imaginations and Practices of Border Making* (Routledge, 2016).
21. On the production methods of the film in such a peculiar context, see Roger Bromley, "Displacement, Asylum, and Narratives of Nation: Giving Voice to Refugees in the Film *La Forteresse*," in *The Culture of Migration: Politics, Aesthetics, and Histories*, ed. Pultz Mosland and Sten Petersen (Bloomsbury, 2015), 51–52.
22. On the discursive and testimonial construction of the asylum seeker's narrative and the display of one's body as evidence of truth, see the classic study by Didier Fassin, *Humanitarian Reason: A Moral History of the Present*, trans. Rachel Gomme (University of California Press, 2011), 83–129.
23. On the forms of persistence and the survival of themes, figures, and forms of pathos from Christian art in humanitarian communication, see Francesco Zucconi, *Displacing Caravaggio: Art, Media, and Humanitarian Visual Culture*, trans. Zakiya Hanafi (Palgrave Macmillan, 2018), especially 27–54.
24. On the controversial notion of secularization, see, for example, Talal Asad, *Formations of the Secular: Christianity, Islam, Modernity* (Stanford University Press, 2007).
25. This notion of biopolitics was encapsulated by Giorgio Agamben through the articulation between the notions of *zoē* and *bios* and

identified in the figure of the "homo sacer." Due to the impossibility of delving here into a vast philosophical and political debate, see Giorgio Agamben, *Homo Sacer: Sovereign Power and Bare Life,* trans. Daniel Heller-Roazen (Stanford University Press, 1998).

26. Michel Foucault, *The Archaeology of Knowledge,* trans. A. M. Sheridan Smith (Routledge, 2002), 35.
27. On the discursive forms and veridical regimes of asylum claims, see Stefano Jacoviello and Tommaso Sbriccoli, "The Case of S.: Elaborating the 'Right' Narrative to Fit Normative/Political Expectations in Asylum Procedure in Italy," in *Cultural Expertise and Litigation: Patterns, Conflicts, Narratives,* ed. Laura Holden (Routledge, 2011), 172–94.
28. For a reconstruction of the political context at the film's release, as well as for a critical reflection on the idea of "non-militancy," see Séverine Graff, "Sans populisme, ni militantisme: Représentation du migrant dans 'La Forteresse' de Melgar," *Décadrages* 14 (2009): 39–50. Translation is mine.
29. Bill Nichols, *Introduction to Documentary* (Indiana University Press, 2001), 110.
30. Nichols, 110.
31. On this point, see again Bromley, "Displacement, Asylum, and Narratives of Nation," 55–57.
32. Daniele Dottorini, *La passione del reale: Il documentario o la creazione del mondo* (Mimesis, 2018), 130. Translation is mine.
33. For a study that assesses the impact of the film in the Swiss and European public sphere, see Philippe Gonzalez and Fabienne Malbois, "Opening *The Fortress:* The Work of Public Gaze on the Swiss Asylum Reality," *Javnost—The Public* 22, no. 1 (2015): 73–91.

4. Embodied Borders and Customized Bodies

1. Emmanuel Carrère, "Letter to a Woman of Calais," in *97,196 Words: Essays,* trans. John Lambert (Farrar, Straus and Giroux, 2019), 287.
2. George's full-length films shot in Calais are *The Impossible: Pieces of Fury* (*L'impossible—Pages arrachées,* 2009), *May They Rest in Revolt: Figures of War* (*Qu'ils reposent en révolte—Des figures de guerres 1,* 2010), and *Fragments* (*Les éclats—Ma gueule, ma révolte, mon nom,* 2011). Among the short films I mention *They Will Kill All of Us* (*Ils nous tueront tous,* 2009), *The Dark Clouds* (*Les nuées,* 2012), and *Nocturne White Hunter* (*Nocturne Blanc-Chasseur,* 2015).
3. The scientific literature on the border area near Calais is vast, and I limit myself here to mentioning Yasmin Ibrahim, "Imaging the Jungles of Calais: Media Visuality and the Refugee Camp," *Networking Knowledge* 9, no. 4 (2016): 1–22; and Dan Hicks and Sarah Mallet, *Lande: The Calais "Jungle" and Beyond* (Policy Press, 2019). For a volume that holds together theoretical and critical contributions and artistic documentation, see Samuel Laquette and Delphine Le

Vergos, eds., *Décamper: De Lampedusa à Calais, un livre de textes et des images & un disque pour parler d'une terre sans accueil* (La Découverte, 2016).

4. Among George's theoretical and critical writings, I mention here "Le peuple qui vient: Gestus du cinéma prophétique," in *Le cinéma critique: De l'argentique au numérique, voies et formes de l'objection visuelle, ed.* Nicole Brenez and Bidhan Jacobs (Éditions Presses de la Sorbonne Nouvelle, 2010); and the book *Time Bomb—Programme sur le cinéma qui vient* (Noir Production, 2016).
5. Henri Michaux, *La vie dans les plis* (Gallimard, 1972), 104–5.
6. See Michel Foucault, *Power/Knowledge: Selected Interviews and Other Writings, 1972–1977,* trans. Colin Gordon (Harvester, 1980), 194–195.
7. Giorgio Agamben, *"What Is an Apparatus?" and Other Essays,* trans. David Kishik and Stefan Pedatella (Stanford University Press, 2009), 23.
8. Agamben, 19. See also Giorgio Agamben, *Profanations,* trans. Jeff Fort (Zone Books, 2007).
9. The reference is to Giorgio Agamben, *Homo Sacer: Sovereign Power and Bare Life,* trans. Daniel Heller-Roazen (Stanford University Press, 1998), 1–13.
10. See Sylvain George and Temesghen Berhe, "La lettre de Temesghen," *L'Autre* 10, no. 1 (2009): 106–7.
11. Jiewon Baek, "Turning Toward the Other: The Face of Humans, the Face of Things, and the Face of Language in the Documentaries of Sylvain George," *Studies in French Cinema* 16, no. 1 (2016): 61–77.
12. For a survey of the works Mathieu Pernot has been producing with migrants, see Mathieu Pernot, *L'atlas en mouvement,* with two texts by Patrick Bucheron and Roland Recht (MUCEM, 2022).
13. On the specific form of political resistance associated with inhabiting a non-place and thus reintroducing a different temporal and spatial conception into it, see Marie Martin, "La jungle de Calais: Contours d'une utopie cinématographique selon Sylvain George," in *Images, médias, et politique,* ed. Sébastien Denis and Claire Sécail (CNRS Éditions, 2013), 359–68.
14. Richard Mosse, *Incoming* (Mack, 2017).
15. Niall Martin, "As 'Index and Metaphor': Migration and the Thermal Imaginary in Richard Mosse's *Incoming.*" *Culture Machine* 17 (2018): 2. For a broader reflection on Mosse's artistic work, see Miriam Stefania De Rosa, "Off the Grid; Strategie di configurazione mediale tra poetica della congiunzione e politica della griglia," *Comunicazioni Sociali* 3 (2023): 353–64. On the relationship between visibility and sovereignty, see James C. Scott, *Seeing Like a State: How Certain Schemes to Improve the Human Condition Have Failed* (Yale University Press, 1998).
16. On George's cinema as an aesthetic of approachability, see Steffen

Köhn, "Chapter Two: Migrant Experience," in *Mediating Mobility: Visual Anthropology in the Age of Migration* (Columbia University Press, 2016), 53–83. For the development of a reflection on George's cinema that focuses on the idea of approach, understood as "method," "attitude," and "approximation," see Emmanuel Alloa, "Vers Madrid," *Multitudes* 4 (2015): 205–10.

17. Debarati Sanyal, "Calais's 'Jungle': Refugees, Biopolitics, and the Arts of Resistance," *Representations* 139 (2017): 10.
18. Patrick Barrès, "Les topographies de la frontière dans *Qu'ils reposent en révolte* (Sylvain George): Une poétique des 'lieux mêlés,'" in *Filmer les frontières*, ed. Corinne Maury (Presses universitaires de Vincennes, 2016), 120. Translation is mine.
19. For a reflection on George's cinema and the issue of the "aestheticization" of migrant bodies and the border environment, see Gabriel Bortzmeyer, "Ne vois-tu pas que je brûle?," *Trafic* 86 (2013): 74–82.
20. Jacques Rancière, "Eclats de lumière," *Trafic* 86 (2013): 73. Translation is mine. On Rancière's reading of George's cinema, see Andrej Šprah, "The Refugee Issue at the Heart of Political Film," *Maska* 32, nos. 185–86 (2017): 86–92.
21. Rancière, "Eclats de lumière," 73.
22. Beyond the film, on borders as sites of intersectional alliance see Ċetta Mainwaring, "Migrant Agency: Negotiating Borders and Migration Controls," *Migration Studies* 4, no. 3 (2016): 289–308; and Carolin Fischer et al., "Revisiting Borders and Boundaries: Exploring Migrant Inclusion and Exclusion from Intersectional Perspectives," *Migration Letters* 17, no. 4 (2020): 477–85.
23. On the idea of "individuation" as a process concerning the environmental instance, the psychological instance, and the collective instance, see again Gilbert Simondon, *Individuation in Light of Notions of Form and Information*, vol. 1, trans. Taylor Adkins (University of Minnesota Press, 2020), 177–80.
24. I refer again to "La lettre de Temesghen." George mentions Temesghen concerning this sequence in "Burning Fingers, October 15, 2007," in *Qu'ils reposent en révolte (carnet de route)*, October 2011, http://reseau-terra.eu/article1205.html.
25. The documents of the conventions determining the state responsible for examining applications for asylum lodged in one of the Member States of the European Union, and subsequent amendments, are available on the EU official website: https://home-affairs.ec.europa.eu/pages/glossary/dublin-convention_en/. For more information, see also the website of the eu-LISA agency, which operationally manages EURODAC: https://www.eulisa.europa.eu/. For a survey of whether the "first entry rule" has helped assimilate asylum policies with migration control, see Gaia Lott, "The Dublin Convention and the Introduction of the 'First Entry Rule' in the Allocation of Asylum

Seekers in Europe," *Contemporary European History* 32, no. 3 (2022): 1–16. On the field effects of the Dublin Convention, see Maurice Stierl, *Migrant Resistance in Contemporary Europe* (Routledge, 2018).

26. For an insight into this and other sequences in the film, I refer again to George, "Burning Fingers, October 15, 2007."
27. On this point, see Karen Fog Olwig et al., *The Biometric Border World: Technologies, Bodies, and Identities on the Move* (Routledge, 2020).
28. For a reflection on gestures of resistance to cinema, as well as cinema as a gesture of resistance, through a discussion with Sylvain George, see Véronique Campan et al., eds., *Qu'est-ce qu'un geste politique au cinéma?* (Presses universitaires de Rennes, 2019), 147–62.
29. Francis Galton, *Finger Prints* (Palala Press, 2015 [1892]).
30. I am referring to the border mediascape temperature, as discussed and developed in previous chapters.
31. Banu Bargu, *Starve and Immolate: The Politics of Human Weapons* (Columbia University Press, 2014), 16.
32. Bargu, 37–86.
33. Roberto Esposito, "Community, Immunity, Biopolitics," *Angelaki* 18, no. 3 (2013): 87. Specifically on the idea of "affirmative borders," see Nick Vaughan-Williams, *Europe's Border Crisis: Biopolitical Security and Beyond* (Oxford, 2015), 121–51.
34. Achille Mbembe, *Necropolitics*, trans. Steven Corcoran (Duke University Press, 2019), 90–92.
35. Bargu, *Starve and Immolate*, 17.
36. George, "Burning Fingers, October 15, 2007."
37. Sara L. Buckingham et al., "The Roles of Settings in Supporting Immigrants' Resistance to Injustice and Oppression: A Policy Position Statement by the Society for Community Research and Action," *American Journal of Community Psychology* 68 (2021): 269–91. On the need to recognize gestures of resistance to border management technologies as political gestures, see Stierl, *Migrant Resistance*.
38. Sanyal, "Calais's 'Jungle' Refugees," 20.
39. Walter Benjamin, "Theses on the Concept of History," in *Selected Writings, Volume 4: 1938–1940*, ed. Howard Eiland and Michael W. Jennings, trans. Edmund Jephcott et al. (Harvard University Press, 2006), 392.
40. The forms of racialization and violence that are expressed on the body constitute the central theme of Frantz Fanon's *Black Skin, White Masks*, trans. Charles Lam Markmann (Grove Press, 2008). This issue is also covered extensively in Frantz Fanon, *The Wretched of the Earth*, preface by Jean-Paul Sartre, trans. Constance Farrington (Grove Press, 1963), especially the chapter "Colonial War and Mental Disorders," 241–310.
41. Fanon, *The Wretched of the Earth*, 159.
42. On anachronism, see Georges Didi-Huberman, *Devant le temps:*

Histoire de l'art et anachronisme des images (Minuit, 2000). Although closely related to the previous one, the reflection on the idea of "anatopism" is less developed in current literature. I have proposed this idea in Francesco Zucconi, *Displacing Caravaggio: Art, Media, and Humanitarian Visual Culture*, trans. Zakiya Hanafi (Palgrave Macmillan, 2018), 199–206; and in "Montaggio e anatopismo secondo Jean-Luc Godard," *FAMagazine: Ricerche e Progetti Sull'architettura e la Città* 51 (2019): 33–41.

43. For a reflection on George's cinema as being capable of maintaining "a different relationship with temporality. It allows the meeting of the near and the far," see Gabriel Bortzmeyer, "L'état d'incandescence (sur le cinéma de Sylvain George)," *Vacarme* 59, no. 2 (2012): 74. Translation is mine. On the forms of historical temporality present in George's cinema through a comparison with Walter Benjamin's "Theses on the Concept of History," see Marie Martin, "À l'épreuve du feu: Égalité et inégalités dans l'oeuvre de Sylvain George," in *Dire les inégalités: Représentations, figures, savoirs*, ed. Raphaelle Guidée and Patrick Savidan (Presses universitaires de Rennes), 133–42.
44. For a significant exception, which nevertheless identifies its focus in the forms of remediation of sculpture in George's cinema, see Francesca Polacci, "Frammenti e dettagli di 'guerra': S. George documenta Calais," *E/C* 12, no. 24 (2019): 261–76.
45. Especially in *Paris Is a Movable Feast* and *The Impossible: Pieces of Fury*.
46. Leo Steinberg, *Other Criteria: Confrontations with Twentieth-Century Art* (University of Chicago Press, 2007), 377.
47. Georges Didi-Huberman, *La ressemblance par contact: Archéologie, anachronisme, et modernité de l'empreinte* (Minuit, 2008), 156. Translation is mine.
48. See Jacques Derrida, *Margins of Philosophy*, trans. Alan Bass (University of Chicago Press, 1982), 1–28.

5. Spectrology of the Border

1. As pointed out on several occasions, the ways in which different borders are managed are constantly evolving. On the Balkan area, see Sanja Milivojevic, *Border Policing and Security Technologies: Mobility and Proliferation of Borders in the Western Balkan* (Routledge, 2019).
2. For a reconstruction by the authors of the genesis and aesthetic and political orientations of the film, see "Maria Kourkouta et Niki Giannari, 'Traverser les frontières de l'Europe est un acte politique,'" interview, *France Culture*, June 24, 2020, https://www.radiofrance.fr/franceculture/podcasts/par-les-temps-qui-courent/maria-kourkouta-et-niki-giannari-traverser-les-frontieres-de-l-europe-est-un-acte-politique-9542652.

3. Karl Marx and Friedrich Engels, *The Communist Manifesto,* intro. Eric Hobsbawm (Verso Books, 2016).
4. Gabriel Bortzmeyer, "Figures migratoires," *CINETRÉNS* 4 (2018): 69. Translation is mine.
5. Thomas Nail, *Theory of the Image* (Oxford University Press, 2019), 26.
6. Reference is to Jacques Derrida, *Specters of Marx: The State of the Debt, the Work of Mourning, and the New International,* trans. Peggy Kamuf, intro. Bernard Magnus and Stephen Cullenberg (Routledge, 1994).
7. On the scenic forms of Greek theater, see Graham Ley, *A Short Introduction to the Ancient Greek Theater,* rev. ed. (University of Chicago Press, 2006).
8. Françoise Frontisi-Ducroux, *Du masque au visage: Aspects de l'identité en Grèce ancienne* (Flammarion, 1995); and E. Anne Mackay, "The Frontal Face and 'You': Narrative Disjunction in Early Greek Poetry and Painting: Chairperson's Address," in *Acta Classica: Proceedings of the Classical Association of South Africa* (Classical Association of South Africa—CASA, 2001), 5–34.
9. For an overview on Muybridge's work, see David Campany, ed., *Moving with the Times: Eadweard Muybridge* (Tate Publishing, 2010).
10. On this point, see also Raphaël Nieuwjaer and Robert Bonamy, "*Des spectres hantent l'Europe,* Maria Kourkouta et Niki Giannari," *Débordements,* June 6, 2018, https://debordements.fr/Des-spectres-hantent-l-Europe-Maria-Kourkouta-et-Niki-Giannari/.
11. Gilles Deleuze, *Cinema 1: The Movement-Image,* trans. Hugh Tomlinson and Barbara Habberjam (University of Minnesota Press, 1986), 2. For a take on Deleuze's investigation of the film machine in relation to the theme of the trace, see Bernard Stiegler, *Technics and Time, 3: Cinematic Time and the Question of Malaise* (Stanford University Press, 2010).
12. Aristotle, *Physics* 6.9, http://classics.mit.edu/Aristotle/physics.6.vi.html.
13. Thomas Nail, "The Migrant Image," in *Handbook of Art and Global Migration: Theories, Practices, and Challenges,* ed. Burcu Dogramaci and Birgit Mersmann (De Gruyter, 2019), 67. For a reflection on movement, between continuity and discontinuity, starting with Zeno's paradox, see Nail, *Theory of the Image,* 24–26.
14. Without elaborating here on Ai Weiwei's film, I refer to the critical reflection developed in Georges Didi-Huberman, "Hauteurs de vue," *Esprit* 446 (2018): 65–78.
15. On the opposition between profile and frontality as structuring Western visual culture, see Meyer Schapiro, *Words and Pictures: On the Literal and the Symbolic in the Illustration of a Text* (Mouton, 1973), 38–39.
16. On the different forms of representation of migrants within Kourkouta and Giannari's film, understood as forms of reflection on the

relationship between recognition and indeterminacy, see Michel Agier, *L'étranger qui vient: Repenser l'hospitalité* (Seuil, 2018), 129–30.

17. Judith Butler, *Notes Toward a Performative Theory of Assembly* (Harvard University Press, 2015), 11.
18. Butler, 91–94.
19. Gilles Deleuze, *Cinema 2: The Time-Image,* trans. Hugh Tomlinson and Robert Galeta (University of Minnesota Press, 1989), 81.
20. Georges Didi-Huberman and Niki Giannari, *Passer, quoi qu'il en coûte* (Minuit, 2017), 32. Translation is mine.
21. I limit myself here to referring to the project of an "atlas of images" undertaken in 1927 and left unfinished. See Aby Moritz Warburg, *Gesammelte Schriften: Der Bilderatlas Mnemosyne,* ed. Martin Warnke and Claudia Brink (Akademie Verlag, 2000).
22. For a reflection on the relationship between the spatiality and temporality of borders, see the different contributions in Hastings Donnan et al., eds., *Migrating Borders and Moving Times: Temporality and the Crossing Borders of Europe* (Manchester University Press, 2017).
23. Didi-Huberman and Giannari, *Passer, quoi qu'il en coûte,* 50.
24. On the relationship between migration and ghosting, see Jean M. Langford, *Consoling Ghosts: Stories of Medicine and Mourning from Southeast Asians in Exile* (University of Minnesota Press, 2013).
25. Marx and Engels, *The Communist Manifesto,* 2, emphasis added.
26. Derrida, *Specters of Marx,* 176.

6. Participation and Citizenship

1. See Antonio Gramsci, *Prison Notebooks,* vol. 3, ed. and trans. Joseph A. Buttigieg (Columbia University Press, 2007). For a revival of Gramscian discourse, see Edward Said, *Orientalism* (Random House/Vintage Books, 1994).
2. See Shirley A. White, ed., *Participatory Video: Images That Transform and Empower* (Sage, 2003). For a broader horizon on the relationships between creativity, participation and social transformation, see Doris Sommer, *The Work of Art in the World: Civic Agency and Public Humanities* (Duke University Press, 2014).
3. Lilie Chouliaraki and Myria Georgiou, *The Digital Border: Migration, Technology, Power* (NYU Press, 2022), 176.
4. See the project launched in 2017: http://www.zalab.org/projects/formazione-video-s-p-r-r. For the SPRAR system, established in Italy by Act No. 189 of July 30, 2002, abolished by Decree 113/2018 (commonly known as the Salvini Decree), converted into Law 132/2018, and replaced by the SIPROIMI, I refer to the official website managed by Ministry of the Interior: https://www.retesai.it.
5. See http://www.zalab.org/teoria/.
6. David Forgacs, *Italy's Margins: Social Exclusion and Nation Formation Since 1861* (Cambridge University Press, 2014), 11.

7. For a historical and theoretical investigation, see David Brancaleone, *Cesare Zavattini's Neo-realism and the Afterlife of an Idea: An Intellectual Biography* (Bloomsbury Publishing, 2021).
8. As an emblematic text regarding the establishment of the idea of democratization in the context of media theory and practice at the turn of the new millennium, see Henry Jenkins, *Convergence Culture: Where Old and New Media Collide* (New York University Press, 2006). On the idea of participation through new media, see Henry Jenkins, *Fans, Bloggers, and Gamers: Exploring Participatory Culture* (New York University Press, 2006).
9. Stefania Parigi, *Fisiologia della percezione: Il pensiero di Cesare Zavattini* (Lindau, 2006), 14. Translation is mine.
10. Unpublished typescript preserved at the Cesare Zavattini Archive in Rome–Reggio Emilia, cited and commented on in Parigi, 71. Translation is mine.
11. See Tullio Masoni and Paolo Vecchi, "Zavattini o dell'incompiutezza: L'esperienza dei cinegiornali liberi," in *Cinenotizie in poesia e prosa: Zavattini e la non-fiction* (Lindau, 2000), 13–23.
12. Cesare Zavattini, "Agli amici del direttivo 'Cinegiornali liberi,'" June 20, 1969, in *Selected Writings,* vol. 1, trans. and ed. David Brancaleone (Bloomsbury, 2021), 363.
13. Zavattini, 362.
14. I refer to the critical essays published in Giorgio Mastinu and Francesca Pola, eds., *Macroradici del contemporaneo: Zavattini inedito* (Electa, 2009). On Zavattini's work as a "complex intermedial montage across literature, cinema, radio, and television, but also including comics and photo-novels," see Nicola Dusi, "Introduzione," in Cesare Zavattini, *Soggetti cinematografici mai realizzati,* ed. Nicola Dusi and Mauro Salvador (Marsilio, 2022), xxvi. Translation is mine.
15. Cesare Zavattini, *La macchina del 2000,* in *Cinema Illustrazione,* February 4, 1931, mentioned in Parigi, *Fisiologia della percezione,* 48. The question is taken up again in "The Imola Conference (1942)," in Zavattini, *Selected Writings,* vol. 1, 37.
16. Cesare Zavattini, "Introduction to the *Cinema Nuovo* Photographic Stories (1955)," in *Selected Writings,* vol. 1, 218–19.
17. Alexandre Astruc, "The Birth of a New Avant-Garde: La caméra-stylo," in *The New Wave,* ed. Peter Graham (British Film Institute, 1968), 17–23.
18. Dziga Vertov, *Kino-eye: The Writings of Dziga Vertov,* trans. Kevin O'Brien (University of California Press, 1984).
19. On this aspect, see again Parigi, *Fisiologia della percezione,* 42.
20. On the contribution and legacy of Zavattini's thought on and beyond neorealism, see Carmelo Marabello, "Indici di luoghi, materie di immagini, eterotopie possibili (di isole minori e maggiori, di altri isolamenti e distanze, di prossimità lontane e distinte, cinema di esterni,

immagini di field)," in *Incontro al neorealismo: Luoghi e visioni di un cinema pensato al presente,* ed. Luca Venzi (Ente dello Spettacolo, 2008), 97–99.

21. On this point and for a reflection on the aesthetic horizon in which Zavattini's thought and practice are inscribed, see Roberto De Gaetano, *Il cinema e i film: Le vie della teoria in Italia* (Rubbettino, 2017), 34–38.
22. Silvana Cirillo, ed., *Zavattini parla di Zavattini* (Lerici: Rome, 1980), 94. Translation is mine.
23. Cirillo, 94.
24. Giorgio Agamben, *Means Without End: Notes on Politics,* trans. Vincenzo Binetti and Cesare Casarino (University of Minnesota Press, 2000).
25. See http://www.zalab.org/projects/flying-roots.
26. On the reality of this neighborhood through its representations, see Federica Mazzara, "Redefining Italian Spaces: Piazza Vittorio and Migratory Aesthetics," in *Rome: Modernity, Postmodernity, and Beyond,* ed. Lesley Caldwell and Fabio Camilletti (Legenda, 2018), 119–32. On Piazza Vittorio and its long-term cinematic memory, see Lesley Caldwell, "Piazza Vittorio: Cinematic Notes on the Evolution of a Piazza," in *Rome: Continuing Encounters Between Past and Present,* ed. Dorigen Caldwell and Lesley Caldwell (Ashgate, 2011), 209–26.
27. See Michel Chion, *Audio-Vision: Sound on Screen* (Columbia University Press, 2019). On the importance of voice and sound in contemporary documentary cinema, see Alma Mileto, *La voce del reale: Il rapporto voce-immagine nel cinema documentario* (Mimesis, 2023).
28. On the "indirect free subjective" film shot as a filmic translation of indirect free speech in literature, see Pier Paolo Pasolini, "Il cinema di poesia," in *Empirismo eretico* (Garzanti, 2007), 167–87.
29. See Laura Busetta, "'Do you want to film yourself?': Narrating the Personal and Rewriting Reality in Agostino Ferrente's *Selfie* (2019)," *Studies in Documentary Film* 17 (2023): 99–114.
30. Pietro Montani, *Emozioni dell'intelligenza* (Meltemi, 2020), 71–72. Translation is mine.
31. Gayatri Chakravorty Spivak, "Can the Subaltern Speak?," in *Marxism and the Interpretation of Culture,* ed. Cary Nelson and Lawrence Grossberg (University of Illinois Press, 1988), 271–313.
32. On this point see Gianluca Gatta, "Self-Narration, Participatory Video, and Migrant Memories: A (Re)making of the Italian Borders," in *The Politics of Public Memories of Forced Migration and Bordering in Europe,* ed. Karina Horsti (Palgrave Macmillan, 2019), 101–20.
33. See Camilla Hawthorne, *Contesting Race and Citizenship: Youth Politics in the Black Mediterranean* (Cornell University Press, 2022).
34. On the idea of rethinking legal and political concepts outside the framework defined by current institutional setups, see Daniele

Salerno and Patrizia Violi, eds. *Stranieri nel ricordo: Verso una memoria pubblica delle migrazioni* (Il Mulino, 2020). For a semiotic perspective on social and political potential of memory, see Cristina Demaria and Patrizia Violi, *Reading Memory Sites Through Signs: Hiding into Landscape* (Amsterdam University Press, 2023).

35. See Nagehan Uskan, "Modes of Self-Representation in the Images Collectively Produced by Migrants in Lésbos Island: *Natives of the New World*," in *Refugees and Migrants in Contemporary Film, Art, and Media*, ed. Deniz Bayrakdar and Robert Burgoyne (Amsterdam University Press, 2022), 51–71.
36. Shirley A. White, "Participatory Video: A Process That Transforms the Self and the Other," in White, *Participatory Video*, 65.
37. In addition to Agamben, *Means Without End*, I also refer to Walter Benjamin, *Toward the Critique of Violence: A Critical Edition*, trans. Julia Ng (Stanford University Press, 2021).
38. Gilbert Simondon, *On the Mode of Existence of Technical Objects*, trans. Cecile Malaspina and John Rogove (Univocal, 2016), 135.
39. Gilbert Simondon, "Psychologie du cinéma," in *Sur la technique* (PUF, 2014), 356. Translation is mine.
40. On the idea that it is possible to identify a link between photographic imprint and forms of ethical, legal, and political recognition, see Ariella Azoulay, *The Civil Contract of Photography* (Zone Books, 2008). On the idea of "visual citizenship" with reference to the Italian context, see Leonardo De Franceschi, *La cittadinanza come luogo di lotta: Le seconde generazioni in Italia fra cinema e serialità* (Aracne, 2018). For a reflection on the relationship between migration, citizenship, and the mapping of urban imaginaries, see Farah Polato, "Paesaggi con figure," *Comparative Studies in Modernism* 17 (2020): 87–100.
41. On the historical ability of the migrant to have a transformative impact on urban scenarios, rearticulating the relationships between local and global, see Iain Chambers, *Migrancy, Culture, Identity* (Routledge, 1994). For a reference to the potential of new media, see the new introduction to the Italian edition of that book, Iain Chambers, *Paesaggi migratori: Cultura e identità nell'epoca postcoloniale* (Meltemi, 2019), 15–16.

INDEX

Francesco Zucconi is associate professor of film and media theory at the Iuav University of Venice, a Membre associé at the Centre d'Histoire et de Théorie des Arts, École des Hautes Études en Sciences Sociales (EHESS), and a Fellow at the Institut Convergences Migrations in Paris. He is the author of several books, including *Displacing Caravaggio: Art, Media, and Humanitarian Visual Culture.*